THE EDDING INVITATION HANDBOOK

THE

WEDDING INVITATION HANDBOOK

WORDING

DESIGN

PRINTING

4880 Lower Valley Road • Atglen, PA 19310

Type set in Hoefler Text

ISBN: 978-0-7643-5610-0
Printed in China

PUBLISHED BY SCHIFFER PUBLISHING, LTD.
4880 LOWER VALLEY ROAD
ATGLEN, PA 19310
PHONE: (610) 593-1777; FAX: (610) 593-2002
E-MAIL: INFO@SCHIFFERBOOKS.COM
WEB: WWW.SCHIFFERBOOKS.COM

For our complete selection of fine books on this and related subjects, please visit our website at www.schifferbooks.com. You may also write for a free catalog.

Schiffer Publishing's titles are available at special discounts for bulk purchases for sales promotions or premiums. Special editions, including personalized covers, corporate imprints, and excerpts, can be created in large quantities for special needs. For more information, contact the publisher.

We are always looking for people to write books on new and related subjects. If you have an idea for a book, please contact us at proposals@schifferbooks.com.

TABLE OF CONTENTS

Chapter Three WORDING

ACKNOWLEDGMENTS

I would like to thank the many people who have worked with me at Julie Holcomb Printers for their fine craftsmanship and shared vision, and also the good people at Schiffer Publishing, who bring a similar spirit of creativity, commitment, and precision to their work. My friend Julie Rath of *Yonder Creative* in Sydney, Austalia, first encouraged me to write this book, and I'm glad she did!.

I've greatly enjoyed the acquaintance of the stationers who partner with me by offering my wedding stationery through their stores. I've benefitted professionally and personally from their diverse perspectives on stationery, business, and life. Kathy Davidson of *Paces Papers* in Atlanta, Julie Pauley of *Kate's Paperie* in New York, and Stacey Bush of *Union Street Papery* in San Francisco were kind enough to offer comments on their readings of the first edition of this book in manuscript form. Brenda Moreira of *House & Paper* in South Miami, Florida; Lisa Resnek Wyett of *Mark Harris Stationers* in Newton, Massachusetts; Gail Brill of *Gail Brill Design* in Saranac Lake, New York; Gwen Gasque of *Letter Perfect* in Palo Alto, California; and Andrea Liss of *Hannah Handmade Cards* in Evanston, Illinois, also provided helpful information. Any errors and omissions, however, are my own.

Thanks are due to Joe and Alec for their patience with the incursion of this project into our home life.

And I would like most of all to thank my customers, who allow me the pleasure and the privilege of being an artisan in the twenty-first century.

*E*ven brides and grooms who do not normally concern themselves with the intricacies of correct social behavior or proper form want to understand the customary practices of wedding invitation wording and design. Whether they want a highly designed invitation, or a more traditional one that is also personal and distinctive, brides and grooms want to know what the boundaries and the options are.

Wedding invitation form in wording and design exists to connect invitations to the ceremony which gives them meaning, and to welcome and show respect for family and guests. The practices I describe in this book weren't established by an independent authority. There are differences in opinion on wedding invitation form and etiquette among stationers and among the many writers on the subject, and between communities. Social changes like divorce, the use of *Ms.*, and couples marrying after establishing themselves as independent adults have asked new questions of etiquette, and the modern appetite for fresh design has challenged some of the conventional practices. Where there is general agreement among the stationers I have consulted and among published authorities on etiquette, I present accepted practices. Where there is not agreement, I give you the options, and sometimes, my opinion.

The information in this book comes from my own observations of wedding invitations over thirty-five years of letterpress printing, numerous conversations with stationers and other experts from around the United States, and my readings of every book I could find dealing with the etiquette of wedding invitations. I have tried to be as complete as possible in creating what I hope will be a helpful and thoughtful reference for anyone involved in the planning, design, and printing of wedding invitations.

Chapter One

HOW MANY? HOW MUCH? HOW LONG?

How Many Should We Order?

The Guest List and the Invitation List

CUSTOMARILY, both families share equally in the guest list, regardless of who pays for the wedding. These days the list is often split three ways, with friends of the couple taking up a third of the list and their families each also taking a third. Of course this is all negotiable, and depends on the size of the wedding, where it is located, and family traditions. South Asian families often issue separate invitations from each of the two uniting families, and so two guest lists will be created, one for each invitation, unless everyone will be receiving both invitations. In any case, you will need to make a master guest list for the wedding invitation you are planning, on which each individual is listed separately. When family members supply their lists to the guest list coordinator, they should be sure to include middle names of guests if the envelopes will be addressed formally, titles where appropriate, and complete addresses, including zip codes. Remember to always include spouses of married guests.

It can take some time to establish your guest list, and the discussions involved may lead to a reappraisal of the size of your wedding. All this has to be settled before you can put together an invitation list and arrive at a figure for the number of invitations you will need to order. Also, if fewer guests will be invited to the ceremony than to the reception, you will need to create a list for each event, so that you will be able to calculate the number of ceremony cards to order in addition to reception invitations. If you will also be sending announcements to a larger circle of acquaintances than you can invite to your wedding, you will need to collect names for a list of those to whom they will be sent as well. Wedding invitations often include enclosure cards inviting guests to ancillary events, such as a welcome dinner, farewell brunch, or henna party. If all guests will not receive an enclosure inviting them to a particular event, you will need to create separate lists and be very careful when stuffing your addressed envelopes. Separate invitations may also be created and sent for each of these events, especially if they are not hosted by the hosts of the wedding.

To calculate the number of invitations you need, you will need to convert your guest list to an invitation list. An entry on the invitation list will represent one invitation, but sometimes more than one individual from the guest list. A couple will be one entry on the invitation list, but represent two entries from the guest list; an entry for a family might represent four. If your guest list is composed of almost all couples and families, and each single person will be invited to bring a guest, you may need fewer than half the number of invitations as there will be invited guests. If many of your guests are single, and they will not be invited to bring guests, you will need a quantity of invitations closer to the number of guests. If you can, add individual invitations for children over thirteen, and don't forget to include your immediate families, the wedding party and their spouses, fiancés or dates, and the officiant and spouse.

Most wedding invitation companies offer stationery items in increments of 25, with a minimum order quantity, usually fifty. Order at least ten more than the total number of entries on your invitation list, to make sure you have a keepsake and for last minute additions to the list. It will cost you much less to order an additional increment of twenty-five invitations now than to reorder a minimum quantity reprinted later.

You should order more envelopes than the number of invitations you will be mailing, to allow for errors in addressing them. If you are using a calligrapher or machine calligraphy (see page 7), you should ask how many extra envelopes they will require. Ten or fifteen percent above the number of finished addressed envelopes is reasonable.

A and B Lists

If your wedding is small, and you have a "B" list of people you would love to invite if there were room, you might send your invitations out ten (or more) weeks before the wedding instead of the usual eight. That way, as guests reply you should still have time to send out additional invitations to replace each regret you receive. You will need to order extra invitations and reply cards if you choose to do this, but it's hard to say how many. You can usually expect around ten percent of invited guests to decline, but you might receive more regrets if many guests will need to travel long distances to attend.

Another way to do this is to order two sets of reply cards, one set with an earlier reply date. Invitations to "A" list guests are sent out ten weeks ahead of the wedding date, with response cards requesting a reply at least six weeks before the wedding. As you receive regrets from the "A" list, you send invitations to "B" list guests, using reply cards with the later reply date. To make this work, you need to order a larger number of invitations to accommodate the second mailing, as well as a second, smaller set of response cards with the later reply dates.

Whichever tactic you use, you risk causing hurt feelings if people discover themselves to have been on the B, rather than the A, list, so it is important that from the beginning of your plans you let people know that your wedding will be very small. This is an important thing to do whenever a small wedding is planned, whether or not the A and B list strategy will be attempted. Many would advise you to not use A and B lists, regardless of the size of your wedding, because the chances of guests finding out and being hurt or offended are just too great. The greater chance of discovery lies with the strategy using two sets of reply cards, with different reply dates.

How Much Will They Cost?

Before you set your wedding stationery budget, take a look at what's available and what the prices are. Some authorities suggest that your invitations should represent some particular percentage of your overall wedding budget, but I find that advice to be arbitrary and unhelpful. Your wedding invitations won't necessarily cost any more because you're having a formal dinner rather than a cocktail reception, nor will they cost any less because you got a great deal on a dress, your brother the pastry chef will be baking the cake, and your sister's band will provide the music. Just because a certain sum happens to be a prescribed percentage of your total wedding budget doesn't mean that you will find anything you like in that price range, or that you will necessarily have to spend that much, either. If your wedding or reception will take place at an expensive, lavishly decorated venue, with elaborate catering, etc., your invitations will likely be a small part of your expenditures. Wedding invitations might be a bigger proportion of the budget for a more modest wedding of a real paper lover, for whom the stationery will be an important personal expression.

The factors that most affect the price of your wedding invitations will be the printing method and quality of materials, the complexity of design (such as multiple colors), the size of your invitation, the number of items of wedding stationery you include, and the quantity of invitation sets you order. It will cost more to have a calligrapher create the text for your wedding invitations than to have your text set in type. An inexpensive style of wedding invitation on thin paper with many pieces and embellishments can end up costing more than the same quantity of less complicated invitations with higher quality printing and paper.

There is a very wide range of prices and quality available for each printing method, but in general, you can expect letterpress, engraving or foil-stamping to cost about 40% more than thermography, and thermography will be about 40% more than offset or digital printing. The current low end of the wedding invitation price range is about $300 for one hundred invitations with printed envelopes and response card sets, with the midrange starting at about $600 to $1000 for those items (keep in mind that a mass-produced greeting card not customized for you at all, and without your return address printed on the envelope or an enclosed reply card set, can cost up to $8). "High end" wedding invitations start at about $1500 for one hundred invitations with printed envelopes and response card sets, going on up to several multiples of that figure. The lowest end of the price range will be digitally printed on inexpensive paper, and the high end will combine more labor-intensive production with higher quality materials.

Prices for professional calligraphy vary regionally from about $2.00 to $10.00, or more, per envelope, with some calligraphers charging by the line. Some calligraphers or stationers will stuff and stamp your invitations for an additional charge.

Envelope lining may be available from the company that prints your invitations. Many stationers are able to line envelopes, and you can also do it yourself (see the Appendix). Envelope lining prices vary a lot, but you can expect that they will add about another two to five dollars per envelope, depending on the supplier and the liner paper you choose.

How Long Will It Take?

Wedding invitations are now usually mailed eight weeks before the wedding, maybe ten weeks in the summer for a fall wedding, since many recipients may be out of town on vacation at that time. If you are using A and B lists and/or planning a destination wedding, you may want to mail your invitations even earlier. You will need to work backwards from your mail date to set a timeline and deadlines for all the stages of the process, from planning and printing to stuffing addressed envelopes.

Printing or Engraving

The usual turnaround time for invitations from established wedding invitation companies is one to two weeks, or up to six weeks for some smaller companies, with digital printing possibly shipping within a few days. Local printers and engravers usually have turnaround times of one to three weeks, depending on their workload at the time, and they may need more time if special papers or envelopes must be ordered for your invitations. Some companies add up to two weeks to the turnaround time to add edging to invitations and other cards (see *Edgings*, p. 86-87). These blocks of time come after you have submitted your text and made all your design decisions and returned approved proofs to the printer. How long you take getting to that point will be a large part of the total time it takes to get your invitations done and in the mail, from start to finish. If you work with a custom wedding invitation designer, your timeline will need to include additional weeks or even months for producing your invitations, so start early.

Most invitation companies can speed up the delivery time for a rush charge. You may also be able to order your envelopes ahead and start addressing them while the invitations are being printed. There will be a small additional charge and additional freight for this, but if this option is offered it will cost considerably less than rushing the whole order.

Don't cut things too close. With all best intentions on the part of everyone involved, sometimes not everything goes exactly as planned, and it may take some additional time to fix things. A company that takes six weeks to deliver your invitations in the first place will be unlikely to be able to fix a mistake instantly.

Using a Calligrapher to Address Your Envelopes

If you have the budget to use a calligrapher, you should plan for plenty of time for his or her work. Many fine calligraphers are booked many months ahead, so make contact with yours as early as you can. Find out how much time your calligrapher will need to complete the addressing of your envelopes, and add on to that the time you or they will need to assemble, stuff, stamp, and mail your invitations. Work backwards from the date your invitations should be mailed and set a deadline for delivery of your printed envelopes to the calligrapher. Don't forget to actually book the time with the calligrapher. Don't just assume they will have time to address your envelopes whenever you present them.

If you will be using place cards and would like the same calligrapher to inscribe them with your guests' names, be sure to book that time when you arrange for your envelopes to be addressed.

Assembling, Stuffing, Stamping, Tying Bows, and Lining Envelopes

After you receive your invitations, they will need to be addressed, assembled, stuffed, and mailed. Below are estimates of how long it may take to do these things yourself; if you are hiring someone else to do any or all of this, find out well in advance how long they will need, book their time, and make sure earlier steps in the process will be completed when they need to be to allow time for this last step.

Kathy Davidson of *Paces Papers* in Atlanta provides these time estimates:

four to six hours	to address 100 envelopes (both inner & outer)
two to three hours	to assemble, stuff, stamp, and seal 100 invitation sets
two to three hours	to tie 100 bows *(don't worry, you'll get the hang of it after the first 3 to 5)*
two to three hours	to line 100 envelopes *(See instructions in the Appendix)*

Don't try to address all the envelopes in one long sitting, or your fatigue may show in the quality of the penmanship. The bridal party or another committee of friends will probably be happy to get together to make quick work of assembling, stuffing, stamping, and sealing your invitations.

Allow yourself at least a week or two for these last steps, or more for a large quantity of invitations. A stationer or calligrapher may need three or four weeks, depending on the number of invitations and how much you ask them to do.

Chapter Two

THIS chapter presents an overview of the many possible components of wedding stationery without going into details of wording or design. It is intended to help you make an informed selection of what to include in your overall design plan and budget. Although you won't be sending items like menus, program covers, and place cards with your invitations, you will want to keep them in mind as you choose or create a design for your wedding invitation.

For complete information on the wording of the stationery items mentioned below, see Chapter Three, and see Chapter Four for information on design.

The Invitation

A traditional wedding invitation is a rectangular card or folder, about 5" x 7", but often somewhat larger, and occasionally smaller. In the past, folders were considered to be more formal than cards, but that is no longer the case. Square cards, multipaneled folders, or very large or unusually shaped (diecut) cards are all possible variations. It will cost more to mail square or extra large invitations, but any invitation with enclosures will probably cost more than an ordinary letter anyway.

Very traditional, and now decidedly old-fashioned as well, is the double-fold invitation. This invitation is a large single-fold invitation, which is folded again (after printing or engraving) to fit into a smaller envelope. To the contemporary eye, the second crease may seem to blemish a beautiful invitation.

Invitation Tissues

Engraved invitations were originally delivered to customers interleaved with tissues to keep the ink from smearing. Engraving inks used to dry more slowly than they do today, and since the lettering is raised, the damp ink could be easily smeared. Although it was never the intention of the engraver, customers often kept the tissues with the invitations when they mailed them to their guests, and the practice became customary. Modern engraving inks dry very quickly, and haven't needed to be sent from the engraver with tissue interleaving for a long time now. Still, tissues may be sent separately to customers who wish to follow the practice of sending their invitations with tissues. If you want to do this, make sure your engraver can send tissues with the invitations, or arrange to acquire them some other way before you place your order. It has never been the custom to send tissues with letterpress invitations, but it is also not some kind of horrible *faux pas* to use them. I have happily provided either traditional tissues or glassine tissues to my customers who have requested them to accompany their letterpress invitations.

We always ship glassine tissues to interleave our letterpress invitations that also include giclée (a fine art digital printing process) or other digital printing, to keep the digitally-printed ink from rubbing off on adjacent cards in transit, and recommend that the glassine tissues be retained in the individually mailed invitations, to keep the digital ink from rubbing off onto other cards in the suite. This might be necessary with any invitation that includes large areas of digital or offset printing.

Envelopes

Most American wedding invitations are mailed in double envelopes. Following this tradition continues a practice that was originally intended to protect hand-delivered invitations from the abuse of the journey. The much-handled outer envelope with the street address was removed (presumably by the butler) so that the addressee received the invitation enclosed only in the pristine inner envelope, which has the name(s) of the invited guest(s), but not the street address, written on the front (which faces out in the larger envelope). It is a peculiarly American wedding custom (including Latin American), and not a European one. To many Americans, an outer envelope enclosing a slightly smaller, unsealed one containing the invitation itself is an essential element of a proper wedding invitation, and the way the inner envelope is addressed is the conventional method to politely make it absolutely clear whether or not children are invited (see *No Children Request*, page 43), or if the recipient may bring a guest. Formal wedding invitations almost always use double envelopes.

Although they are less traditional, single envelopes are also correct for all weddings. It is certainly less time-consuming to address them, and single envelopes save on both paper and postage. They are also available in more papers than are double wedding envelopes. But since double envelopes are so important to so many people (and probably your mother and/or grandmother), it's a good idea to not make a final choice to use single envelopes until you check with everyone who is participating financially in the wedding invitations, or at least whose feelings about them matter to you. (I've printed double wedding envelopes to replace previously printed single envelopes for wedding invitations more than once.)

Reception Cards

If reception information is not included on the invitation itself, a smaller reception card is enclosed with the invitation. This is never necessary when the reception takes place immediately after the ceremony and in the same location. When the reception is held in a location different from that of the wedding, it is perfectly correct to invite guests to the reception on the wedding invitation, but it is more formal to use a separate reception card. In either case, if the reception information requires several lines of type, you might prefer to use a reception card rather than crowd the invitation.

Ceremony Cards

When a small wedding is followed by a larger reception, the main invitation should invite guests to the reception. Rather than mail a separate invitation to the ceremony, a smaller card is generally enclosed in some of the reception invitations to invite just those guests to the ceremony.

Mormon wedding invitations are invitations to a reception in a home or other location, with smaller ceremony cards enclosed for those guests who may be present in the Temple to attend the wedding ceremony.

Reply Cards

Although a reply card with return envelope is by no means required, and it is always proper to include reply information on the bottom left of an invitation, it has become a solidly customary practice to include a reply set. A one- or two-sided reply postcard is sometimes used instead of a small card with a self-addressed stamped envelope. In either case, a reply card is sometimes used to gather other information from guests, such as their meal selections.

You may also enclose with your wedding invitation a reply card which will not be returned to you. This card includes a reply request, with the address information for the response. Guests are expected to reply with their own notes. Sometimes this kind of reply card request replies via email, possibly along with the address of an informational website set up for the wedding.

Website Cards

Many couples now enclose small cards with their invitations, directing recipients to a website they have created for the convenience of their wedding guests. Sometimes this card requests that guests reply via a wedding website, but a small website card is often included in addition to a conventional reply card with envelope.

Maps and Directions Cards

Many fewer map cards and directions cards are printed now than in the past, since most guests will be able to get this information online. Nonetheless, some locations are not well served by these sources, particularly when the location is not immediately reachable by vehicles, and so couples may decide to include a map and/ or directions card with their invitations. Also, particularly when you are inviting guests to a destination wedding, a map showing locations of various activities can be helpful, and also add a fun graphic element to your suite.

Because of the amount of information included on them, maps or directions cards are usually larger than reply cards but smaller than invitations. Ideally, they should be printed on the same stock and in the same manner as the rest of your invitation set. If you can't afford this, you can choose a nice complimentary paper and have your map and directions digitally printed.

If you would like to use both written directions and a map, you can use two cards, or you can have a two-sided card printed letterpress or digitally. Engraving and thermography cannot be used for two-sided cards, so you will need to include two cards if you want both, or include a card with both a map and directions on the same side.

Accommodations Cards

If many of your guests will be coming from out of town, you may want to have accommodations cards printed to accompany some or all of your invitations. These cards present information about lodgings convenient to the location of your wedding, perhaps with blocks of rooms reserved for your guests, and sometimes also about the closest airport, local transportation, or transportation that you will be providing. This information may also be provided on a wedding website.

Activity Cards and Itinerary Cards

When guests are invited to a destination wedding, or if many guests may be travelling from out of town and staying for the wedding weekend, their hosts may want to inform them of activities and events available during their stay. If these activities will play a role in guests' planning, determining their arrival and departure times or clothing they should bring along, they should be informed well before the wedding. Information can be included on an activity card sent with a save the date card or with the invitation. If guests don't need to know about all the activities ahead of time, you can print itinerary cards which you can present to them at a welcome dinner or cocktail party, or place in welcome baskets sent to their rooms.

Invitations to Welcome Dinners, Farewell Brunches, Etc.

Sometimes all out-of-town guests, or all the wedding guests, are invited to the dinner following the wedding rehearsal, which becomes a welcome dinner rather than a traditional rehearsal dinner attended only by the wedding party and the bride's and groom's families. Invitations to this and other events, such as a kiddush lunch, mehndhi party, wedding day brunch or an after party following the rehearsal dinner, are often included with wedding invitations. If everyone is invited, a line can be added to the invitation reply card where guests may indicate whether or not they can attend a particular event. If only some of the wedding guests are invited, then the enclosure card inviting them to the dinner may include an *R.s.v.p.* and a telephone number or email address at the bottom. Alternatively, two sets of reply cards may be printed, one for guests invited to the ceremony only and one for guests invited to multiple events.

Traditionalists may consider it to be improper to include other invitations with your ceremony and reception invitations, especially if the events are hosted by different individuals; others feel that making things easier for you and for your guests is a thoughtful extension of traditional etiquette. If your invitation seems upstaged or cluttered with multiple enclosure cards, or if it seems to you improper to include them, you will prefer to send separate invitations for events like the rehearsal/ welcome dinner and wedding day brunch, and you will send accommodations and activity information with save the date cards rather than with invitations.

At Home Cards

Small cards giving a couple's address after a certain date are often included in wedding invitations or announcements. In addition to providing their new address, *at home* cards inform friends and families of the couple's names after marriage. It's hard to guess whether a woman will adopt her husband's name or if one or both will adopt a hyphenated form, and some couples now choose an entirely new last name for their married life. Thank you notes are another vehicle for transmitting this information.

Other Enclosure Cards

You may wish to enclose a card which entitles your guest to valet parking, special seating *within the ribbon* or in a particular pew, or admission to your wedding location if uninvited guests may intentionally or unintentionally attend.

Wedding Announcements

Wedding announcements are printed ahead and then mailed by a trusted friend on the day after the wedding. Especially if your wedding is small, you might want to send announcements to friends, relatives, and acquaintances, such as business associates, who weren't included in your wedding, but would like to hear the great news. If your wedding is an elopement, only announcements will be sent. You, or another host, may also choose to send an invitation to a reception celebrating your recent marriage in addition to or instead of an announcement.

If you will be sending both invitations and announcements, it's a good idea to order them at the same time, and in the same or a similar style. If a calligrapher will be addressing your invitation envelopes, you should bring the announcement envelopes to the same person.

Rehearsal Dinner Invitations

A rehearsal dinner is traditionally hosted by the groom's parents, and they issue the invitations. Rehearsal dinner invitations are sometimes enclosed with the wedding invitations (see *Invitations to Welcome Dinners, Farewell Brunches, Etc.*, p.13), although a traditionalist would consider this to be improper, and it is rarely done in the South. Since a small number of people will be attending the rehearsal dinner, the information about this event is frequently conveyed informally, through a handwritten note or telephone call.

Wedding Programs and Program Covers

A program is certainly not necessary for a wedding ceremony, but it can be a keepsake for you and your guests, and honor your wedding party, family members, and other special people in your lives. Programs can be a place to celebrate your community's traditions, and they can be helpful for explaining practices that may be unfamiliar to some guests.

If the contents of your program are extensive, or might change, but you still want a program to match your invitations, it might be best to order a program cover when you order your invitations, and then have the interior pages digitally printed closer to the time of the ceremony. If you use nice paper, digitally printed pages will look fine inside a letterpressed or engraved cover.

Menus

If you wish, you may provide a menu for each guest. Menus may also serve as place cards when they are printed leaving a space for each guest's name to be written in at the top. You will probably want to have your menus match or coordinate with your other wedding stationery.

Seating Cards and Escort Cards

To guide your guests to their assigned tables at your reception, you may provide them with seating cards. These are small cards printed with the words, "*You are seated at table number* ___." and enclosed in envelopes addressed to an individual or couple or a family, or the name(s) of the guests may simply be written on the backs of the cards. Seating cards may be ordered to match or coordinate with your wedding invitations, or purchased in packages from your stationer. It is also fine to use blank cards, and simply write the table number on each one.

The seating card envelopes (or cards, with guests' names facing up) will be arranged in alphabetical order on a table near the entrance to the reception. Instead of seating cards, you can help guests find their seats with an easy-to-read seating chart, or if your wedding is small, guests can circulate around the tables until they spot their place cards.

If you use escort cards, each one will be enclosed in a small envelope addressed to the assigned male escort of the woman whose name appears on the card. These are rarely seen today.

Place Cards and Table Cards

If you assign seats at your dinner reception, you will need a card inscribed with a guest's name at each place setting. Place cards are either flat or tent-folded. They may be plain paper cut to size, or purchased from your stationer, either packaged or custom printed with a design that coordinates with your other wedding stationery. (Menus may also serve as place cards - see *Menus*, above).

If there are many tables, you may help your guests find their way by displaying numbered table cards. Sometimes table cards are named, rather than numbered, often following a location-oriented theme, such as names of places important in the couple's lives, neighborhoods in the city where the wedding takes place, etc. These may either be tent-folded to stand on their own, or you can purchase or rent special stands for them. Your stationer may sell packaged table cards, or you (or your calligrapher) can write numbers on plain or printed cards.

Matches and Napkins

Napkins or matchboxes personalized with your names, initials, monogram or other motif, and your wedding date can be ordered through your stationer.

Other Reception Stationery

Sometimes other *objets de papier* are printed for the wedding reception. You can have favor cards or tags custom printed to match your wedding invitations, or make them for your guests. They may carry your names or initials and the date, a favorite quote, an image also used on other wedding stationery, etc. They may be drilled with holes so they can be attached to your favors with ribbons or ties. Ocasionally bookmarks are printed as favors or favor cards.

Sometimes special cards are printed informing guests of a donation that has been made *In lieu of favors* for the guests, and some couples provide special cards for guests to write notes for mounting as keepsakes in their wedding book.

Save the Date Cards

If your wedding will take place at a time or location that will require your guests to plan well ahead for travel or accommodations, you might consider sending save the date cards six to eight months, or even a year before the event. A save the date card doesn't need to conform exactly to the design of your wedding invitation, but if you do send save the date cards, they will be your guests' first introduction to the event, so you may want to set the style for what is to come.

Enclosures with travel or accommodations information are often included with save the date cards, or the save the date cards are combined with the other information on two- or three-paneled folders.

Engagement Announcements

An engagement is announced to friends and family informally or at an engagement party, and possibly via a newspaper announcement. If there are many people you would like to inform about your engagement who may not be reached by your newspaper announcement, you may wish to send printed or engraved engagement announcements. Traditionally, these are issued by the bride's parents, rather than by the couple or the parents of the groom. An invitation to an engagement party often serves as an announcement. Someone other than the couple hosts the engagement party in their honor.

Shower Invitations
Shower invitations are issued by the hosts of the shower, which are always friends of the bride, groom, or couple, but never the couple themselves, their siblings or parents.

Gift Acknowledgment Cards
Gift acknowledgment cards, promising a later thank you note, are a holdover from a time when wealthy couples might take a long European tour before returning to write thank you notes. Everyone knows that the mail works from everywhere these days, so nothing gets you off the hook from writing actual thank you notes right away. Don't use gift acknowledgment cards to try to buy more time; just write the notes.

Thank You Notes
Thank you notes should be sent as soon as possible, and within two months after gifts are received, at the very latest, so you will need to have some notes as soon as you start receiving gifts. You can buy packaged flat or folded notes or letterpapers, or have personalized ones custom printed. Folding notes are traditionally considered to be most formal. Joint thank you notes printed with both of your names are not traditionally used before you are married. This is certainly true for notes printed with *Mr. and Mrs.*, but it's understandable if long-established couples who already have joint stationery choose to ignore this rule.

First Wedding Anniversary
Don't forget that paper is the traditional first wedding anniversary gift. You can find beautiful packaged stationery, or have personalized letterpaper, calling cards, or note cards printed for your spouse. A first wedding anniversary gift could also be a journal or a book.

Chapter Three

WORDING

CUSTOMARY wedding invitation wording is concise and straightforward, speaking with a warm and dignified voice. The rules support clarity, respect for individuals, and respect for the wedding ceremony. Wedding invitations are keepsakes and important ceremonial documents.

Weddings unite a couple in the supportive presence of invited guests and bring together families, generations, and communities. Wedding invitation wording should reflect and nurture these connections.

Even formal wedding invitations may depart from traditional wording in some ways. In the text below I have provided the hard and fast rules as well as the flexible ones for twenty-first-century American wedding invitations.

Third Person or First Person, but Not Both

Either use the third person (*Mr. and Mrs. Andrew Martyns/request the pleasure of your company*), which is traditional and formal, or use the first person (*Please join us* – with the host[s] listed at the bottom), which is less formal, but don't switch from one to the other (*Andrea Martyns and George Jones/invite you to join us*).

Punctuation and Capitalization

In wedding invitations, a period is used after titles such as *Mr., Mrs.*, and *Ms.*, but not at the end of a line of text. Use a comma before *junior,* but not before *III*, and between the day of the week and the day of the month (*Saturday, the sixth of May*), but not at the end of a line. The line breaks themselves function as punctuation, whether it would be a comma, period, or even semicolon if the invitation were some other kind of prose.

The normal capitalization rules for correct English are followed on wedding invitations. The first letter of the first word of what would be a sentence should be capitalized, such as the first word of the invitation itself, and lines like Reception to follow, or Black tie invited, which are abbreviated sentences. Proper nouns such as the day of the week and the name of the month are also capitalized, but not the day of the month (like *sixth*) or the year. You shouldn't capitalize a.m. or p.m., unless they are part of a line of capitals or small caps. You shouldn't capitalize words at the beginning of lines, unless they begin sentences, or capitalize nouns that aren't proper nouns. Sometimes people are tempted to do this to stress the importance of the event, but it's incorrect to do so, and it makes the text of the invitation look like the words on a theater marquee.

Names and Titles

It is most formal and traditional to use full names, with middle names spelled out. It is less traditional, but no less formal, to omit middle names completely. Middle initials are not customarily used on wedding invitations. Nicknames are never used on formal wedding invitations, and rarely appear even on informal ones.

Titles should be used in the invitation text and in addressing the envelopes for formal wedding invitations. It is correct but less formal to omit titles entirely. The next section discusses the use of titles generally; see also the sections on the host line, presenting the couple, and on addressing envelopes.

Mr. and Mrs. or Ms.

The subject of titles and the associated issues about the order of the names of married couples using titles is a lot more interesting than it used to be. Not so long ago, the only titles a woman ever used were *Mrs.* and *Miss*. There weren't any women senators to worry about. And if a woman did have a title, such as *Dr.* or *Judge*, it wasn't used socially as a man's professional title would be. A male physician was *Dr.* professionally as well as socially, whereas a female physician was *Dr.* professionally but not socially. She was always *Miss*, or *Mrs.* to her husband's *Mr., Dr., Mayor, Judge, Rabbi, Reverend, The Honorable*, etc. As recently as 1993, *Crane's Wedding Blue Book* suggested that a woman who hadn't adopted her husband's name, or was a judge, doctor, or minister, agree to using *Mr. and Mrs.* on her daughter's wedding invitation, with her husband's first and last name.

Now that women do use their professional titles socially just as men do, and often do not adopt their husbands' surnames when they marry, etiquette mavens have been scrambling to guide the writers of wedding invitations and the addressers of envelopes (not just for wedding invitations).

Everyone agrees that the names of married couples are connected by *and,* and listed on the same line unless there isn't room. If the names are long, they are listed in two lines, with the word *and* at the beginning of the second line. If a couple is divorced, their names are always listed in two lines, and not connected by the word *and*. All of this applies equally to same-sex parents.

Ms.

The title *Ms.* is never used with a husband's first and last name, as is done with *Mrs.* Some women adopt their husband's last name or create a hyphenated or completely new last name with their husband and use *Ms.* with their first name and married last name, but you have no way of knowing that she's doing this from her title. *Ms.* supplies no more information about a woman's marital status than does *Mr.* about a man's. That's the point, actually.

Some etiquette writers abandon the traditional order of *Mr. and Mrs. Thomas Hopkins* when a woman retains her name after marriage, invoking the *Ladies First Rule.* According to this point of view, the title *Ms.* reverses the traditional order, causing the woman's name to precede the man's, giving you *Ms. Marjorie Dale and Mr. Thomas Hopkins.* Many stationers are very fond of the *Ladies First* rule.

Other respected etiquette authorities, especially those with backgrounds in diplomacy and protocol, retain the traditional *Mr. and Mrs.* order, simply allowing it to include *Ms.* in place of *Mrs.* The traditional form of *Mr. and Mrs. Thomas Hopkins* is actually a shortened form of *Mr. Thomas Hopkins and Mrs. Thomas Hopkins.* Just change her name, and you get *Mr. Thomas Hopkins and Ms. Marjorie Hopkins* (or *Ms. Marjorie Dale* if she hasn't changed her name*).* You don't need any new rules, because the well-established practice we already have works.

Proponents of both schools of thought agree that the rules of protocol regarding rank should be followed for women as well as men, listing first the spouse of either sex with higher governmental, military, or clerical rank. Most would also include *Dr.* as a professional rank, and list first the spouse who is a doctor. There is also agreement that a married couple may be presented in any order when titles are dropped.

Since respected experts give differing advice for the order of a married couple's names when *Ms.* is used, you may choose. In my opinion, following the *Mr. and Mrs.* rule makes the most sense and so I've used that form throughout this book. It's a simple solution to a simple problem, accommodating change within the traditional practice. Reversing the name order when *Ms.* is used seems to me to have been pulled out of thin air, and quite unnecessarily.

Using a Mother's First Name on a Wedding Invitation

Traditionally, when a married or widowed woman uses *Mrs.*, it is always with her husband's name. According to convention, when a woman uses her first name with *Mrs.*, it means she is divorced.

Following these conventions, if the married mother of the bride wishes her first name to appear on her daughter's wedding invitation, she cannot use the title *Mrs.* without appearing to be divorced. If she uses the title *Ms.*, her first name appears, and if all titles are dropped, a woman who normally uses the title of *Mrs.* uses her first name, appearing with her husband as *Thomas and Charlotte Winslow* or *Charlotte and Thomas Winslow*.

Many will find quite reasonable the South Asian practice of including a woman's first name when using *Mr. and Mrs.*, so *Mr. Yash and Mrs. Bhavna Parmar*, for example. This follows an Indian practice of referring to a married couple as *Shri Yash and Shrimati Bhavna Parmar* (with the spelling of the titles varying according to region). Either *Mr. and Mrs.* or *Shri and Shrimati*, or the couple's names without titles, are properly used for couples of South Asian heritage on wedding invitations (and in addressing envelopes).

I have reprinted reply envelopes that had been ordered by the couple with the mother of the bride as the return addressee, innocently using *Mrs.* with her first name and her husband's last name, and so making her appear to some to be divorced, when she was not. Fortunately, in this case, the *faux pas* was discovered before the invitations were stuffed and mailed. To avoid possible misunderstanding, the type was reset, and the reply envelopes reprinted. The real lesson here is this: *show your wedding invitation proofs to your parents, all of them, before you approve the proofs*. Using your mother's first name with *Mrs.* might not seem important to you, but it might matter to her.

Doctor

It is most formal to spell out *Doctor*, but *Dr.* is also correct, and wise, if the names already make a long line.

When both members of a married couple are doctors, they may be referred to as *The Doctors Petrovsky* or as *Dr. Richard Petrovsky and Dr. Maria Petrovsky*. If one member is a doctor and the other is not, substitute *Dr.* for *Mr., Mrs.,* or *Ms.* and list the name of the spouse who is a physician first.

Dr. and Mrs. Jon Smith

or

Dr. Jon Smith and Ms. Marjorie Hancock

or

Dr. Marjorie Smith and Mr. Jon Smith

Appellations such as M.D., D.D.S., and Ph.D. are not used on wedding invitations. If a holder of an academic degree is normally referred to as Dr., that title may be used on a wedding invitation, but generally it is not, except in the case of *Reverend Doctor.*

Junior

The designation *junior* is not capitalized when spelled out, but is when abbreviated as *Jr.*

Esquire

The title *Esquire* or *Esq.* is not used on a wedding invitation.

Special Titles for Elected Officials, Clergy, and Members of the Military

See the APPENDIX for information on listing names with these kinds of titles.

The Invitation

Sacred Text or Poetry

You may may wish to honor the sanctity of the wedding ceremony with sacred words at the top of your wedding invitation, or at the bottom. Jewish invitations usually place the Hebrew letters *bet hay* in the upper right hand corner of the card to signify the holiness of the document. Hindu wedding invitations often place the words *Om Shree Ganeshaya Namah* at the top of the card, and invitations following Islamic traditions may present words from the Qur'an, in beautiful Arabic calligraphy, above the text of the invitation. A verse from the Bible is sometimes printed at the top or bottom of a Christian wedding invitation. All of these, and also words of poetry, are perfectly appropriate as part of a wedding invitation.

Host Line(s)

Traditional wedding custom assumes that the parents of the bride pay for the wedding and are therefore the hosts. As the hosts, they are inviting the guests, and so their names appear in the first line of the wedding invitation text. Whether or not they are paying for all or part of the wedding, a bride may wish to honor her parents in this way.

A couple may wish to honor the groom's parents, or acknowledge their financial contribution to the wedding, by adding their names after the bride's parents names, following the word *and* or the phrase *together with* on a line that separates the two sets of parental names. Hispanic heritage wedding invitations almost always include parents of both the bride and the groom at the top of the invitation. It is also common for the names of the groom's parents to be included on a line following the groom's name, preceded by *son of.* The inclusion of the groom's parents in this way has long been customary in Jewish families, but it's a new practice for other traditions.

Invitations for Indian weddings (and also other traditions, such as Dutch) customarily honor grandparents and possibly other relatives by including them as hosts, and they may emphasize that an entire family is hosting by adding lines at the bottom of the card, with names of additional family members, following *"With the compliments of"* or *"With best wishes from"*. There can be two sets of invitations for Indian weddings, one version from the groom's family to their guests, and the other from the bride's family to their guests.

Whether or not the couple is carrying the full expense of the wedding, they may feel that it is most appropriate that they be the hosts of their wedding, or they may wish to invite guests *together with their families*. When they host as a couple, the bride's name precedes the groom's, and they use their full names with titles, or they both use full names without titles.

DIVORCED PARENTS

Things can get complicated if one or both parental couples have divorced, and even more so if any have remarried. If no stepparents are included, the divorced parents' names are listed on separate lines, without the connecting word *and*. It is no longer considered to be improper to include stepparents on wedding invitations, and the spouse may be listed in the same line with the parent, but listing everybody can crowd the wedding invitation, especially if the names are long and you would like to include all the parents of both the bride and the groom. In this case, and also when there is a risk of creating an awkward situation by including or omitting particular individuals, having the couple host the wedding *together with their families* becomes especially appealing, if not the only possible solution. (*Together with their families* or, alternatively, *together with their parents*, may either precede or follow the couple's names.) On the other hand, some people have happily told me that their wedding invitations were the one place where all of their parents could appear together, at least in typographic proximity. So do what's best for your family.

Etiquette experts agree that the bride's divorced mother should precede her ex-husband on their daughter's wedding invitation. If she has remarried and uses the title *Mrs.*, and is hosting with her husband, this means that she actually appears second, after her new husband, but still ahead of her ex-husband, the bride's father.

This is not an ancient tradition, but a relatively recent effort to prevent modern family squabbles by setting a rule, which can be seen as arbitrary and therefore fair, or as honoring the traditional role of the mother of the bride as the planner of her daughter's wedding. What about a groom's divorced mother? To be consistent, she, or she and her new husband, will be listed on a separate line placed ahead of the groom's father's name (and his new wife's, if there is one) when they are included on a wedding invitation. When more than one set of parents is listed for either one, you will need to include the last names of the bride and groom on the invitation. Remember that divorced parents' names are not connected by *and*.

DIVORCED PARENTS, NOT REMARRIED, OR HOSTING WITHOUT SPOUSES

Mrs. (or *Ms.) Marjorie Dale Hopkins* (or *Ms. Marjorie Elaine Dale)*

Mr. Thomas James Hopkins

request the honour of your presence

at the wedding of their daughter

DIVORCED PARENTS, REMARRIED AND HOSTING WITH SPOUSES

Mr. and Mrs. Henry Robert Martin

(or *Mr. Henry Martin and Ms. Marjorie Elaine Dale)*

Mr. and Mrs. Thomas James Hopkins

request the honour of your presence

at the wedding of Mrs. Martin's (or *Ms. Dale's) and Mr. Hopkins's daughter*

(both bride's and groom's full names are listed, since last names may not be obvious)

DIVORCED AND REMARRIED PARENTS OF BOTH BRIDE AND GROOM HOSTING
(The first couple listed in each case includes the mother of the bride or groom)

Mr. Henry Martin and Ms. Marjorie Elaine Dale
(or Mr. and Mrs. Henry Robert Martin)
Mr. and Mrs. Thomas James Hopkins
and
Mr. and Mrs. Robert Sarkissian
Mr. and Mrs. Frederick Howard Allston
request the pleasure of your company
at the marriage of

(both bride's and groom's full names are listed, since last names may not be obvious)

SEPARATED PARENTS

Separated parents are listed on separate lines, just as divorced parents are, except that if the woman adopted her husband's name when she married, according to convention her name is still most correctly stated using the title *Mrs.* followed by her husband's full name (since she is still married to him). If she is not comfortable with this, she may be listed with her own full name following either *Mrs.* or *Ms.*

WIDOWED PARENT

If one of your parents is widowed and remarried, and both parent and stepparent host, guests are usually invited to the wedding of *his* or *her* (rather than *their*) daughter. Make your own call on this. It depends largely on your relationship with your stepparent. If you are very close to your stepparent, you may abandon that formality, and be *their* daughter on your wedding invitation if you wish.

The following example does not imply any antipathy toward Andrea's step-mother, but this wording would be disrespectful and unkind to the bride's mother in the case of a divorce, unless perhaps when the parent missing from the wedding invitation was deceased, or had been truly missing from the bride's life for a very long time.

WIDOWED PARENT HOSTING WITH SPOUSE

Mr. and Mrs. Robert Washington
request the pleasure of your company
at the marriage of Mr. Washington's daughter
Andrea Jeanne

DECEASED PARENT

Many traditionalists firmly believe that a deceased parent should never be listed on a wedding invitation. I believe that you may include him or her on the invitation in some way, even if it's important in your tradition that a deceased parent doesn't appear to be hosting the wedding.

In the Jewish tradition, the name of a deceased parent may be indicated by a Star of David above the name, or by the abbreviated Hebrew phrase meaning *may his/her name be a blessed memory,* instead of being preceded by the words *the late* (see page 109 in the PORTFOLIO OF SAMPLES). In Hispanic heritage wedding invitations, a deceased parent is sometimes listed as a host, indicated by a small cross or Star of David above the name.

Son of the late, or *son of Angela Liu and the late Ray Liu* following the groom's name always works, but it's awkward to add a *daughter of* line after the bride's name unless the couple is hosting. If the couple is not hosting, and the couple would like to honor the bride's deceased parent, this is when a mention on the wedding program, or even an enclosure card may be the most appropriate way. I've printed enclosures indicating that *in lieu of favors,* the couple has made a donation in the memory of the bride's mother.

Amy Elizabeth Johnson
daughter of
Mr. Richard Johnson and the late Mrs. Richard Johnson
and
Michael Hudson Phillips
son of
Dr. and Mrs. James Phillips
request the honour or your presence
at their wedding

or

Mr. and Mrs. Richard Johnson
request the honour or your presence
at the marriage of their daughter
Amy Elizabeth Johnson
to
Michael Hudson Phillips
son of
the late Dr. James Phillips

ADOPTIVE PARENTS

Of course, your adoptive parents invite guests to the wedding of *their daughter* or *son*. If you are particularly close to your natural parent(s), you might want to honor them in a wedding program, or they might host a party in your honor, but you are not obligated to find a place for them on your wedding invitation, except in the all-inclusive *together with their families*.

Request Line

It is traditional to *request the honour of your presence* at a wedding held in a place of worship, and to *request the pleasure of your company* at a wedding held anywhere else. Of course, you may depart from custom and invite your guests with one of many variations on that theme, such as: *invite you to join them/in the joyous celebration of their wedding; would be delighted by your presence at the wedding of; request your presence as holy witnesses at the marriage ceremony of;* etc.

The words *honor* and *favor* have long been traditionally used with the English spellings, *honour* and *favour*, on wedding invitations, and both spellings are equally correct and equally formal. The important thing is to be consistent, using either the American form or the English form throughout.

Wedding is probably the most common word used for the marriage event, but that varies by tradition. Most Hispanic heritage wedding invitations will use *marriage*, and that word is used more often than *wedding* in some other traditions as well.

REQUEST LINES FOR CATHOLIC WEDDINGS

If you will be married in a Nuptial Mass, you should let your guests know, so that they will be prepared for the duration of the ceremony. The hosts will *request the honour of your presence/at the Nuptial Mass uniting/*(the bride *and* the groom)*/in the Sacrament of Holy Matrimony.*

Recipient Line

The most formal printed wedding invitations leave a space for the handwritten name of the recipient. It's a lovely custom, rarely followed today. It's a more expensive option, since, unless you or someone close to you has truly beautiful handwriting, you need to hire a calligrapher to inscribe each invitation with the full name (no initials) of the recipient(s), possibly the calligrapher who provides art for the names of the bride and groom, which would be printed with the rest of the text. You'd want to design the invitations so that the recipient's name doesn't become the main focus of the invitation. That position should go to the couple.

Mr. and Mrs. Harold Sorensen
request the honour of

Mr. and Mrs. James Wilkinson's

presence at the marriage of their daughter

or

The pleasure of the company of

Ms. Charlene Hunt Greerson

is requested at the marriage of

Presentation of the Couple

In the most traditional wedding invitations, the bride's name is almost never preceded by a title, and the groom's name is always preceded by *Mr.*, or another title, such as *Doctor.* Traditional formal etiquette would confer the title of *Miss* on the bride in the unusual event that the parents of the groom issue the invitations, or foist the title of *Mrs.* upon her if she has been married before (*Mrs. Amanda Fish* if she's divorced; *Mrs. Andrew Fish* if she's a widow).

Contemporary usage generally treats both members of the couple equally with respect to titles, usually dropping or including them for both, although it's not uncommon to see the title *Mr.* for the groom with no title for the bride. If a woman normally uses a professional title such as *Doctor* or *Judge* or holds a military rank, she may definitely use it on a formal wedding invitation, and she may also use *Ms.* (rarely *Miss*) if a title is used for the groom. She never has to use *Mrs.*, regardless of the circumstances of her previous marriage.

Customarily, a formal invitation presents first the bride, followed by the name of the groom, separated by a line containing the word *and, to,* or *with.* Same-sex wedding invitations generally present the couple in alphabetical order. The parents of a bride may invite you to the wedding or marriage of their daughter *and* the groom, or to the wedding/marriage of their daughter *to* the groom. The first wording places the emphasis on the couple, and the second places the emphasis on the bride, which is more traditional, but no more formal. Jewish weddings always use *and* as the connecting word.

If you wish to place the bride and groom on absolutely equal standing, or if you just like how it looks, you may also list them on the same line, with or without titles, the bride followed by the groom, or in alphabetical order for a same-sex couple, connected by the word *and* or *to.* This is a nontraditional practice, since traditional etiquette permits only married couples to be listed on the same line, connected by *and.* If titles and full names are used throughout the invitation and *Black tie* appears at the bottom, the invitation will be accepted by most people as formal nonetheless.

If the bride's parents are hosting the wedding, and her last name may be taken to be obvious from their names, her last name is omitted. If her last name isn't obvious from their names, it should be stated. Both the bride's and the groom's last names are usually stated if both the bride's and the groom's parents are hosting.

Date and Time Lines

The day of the week is followed by the day of the month in one line, the year is spelled out in the next line, and then the time of the ceremony is given in a third line. The date line may begin with *on,* or the preposition may be omitted; the time line usually begins with *at.* It is more formal to spell out all the numbers. The day and month are always capitalized, but the year, if included, should not be. The year was never capitalized on invitations in the past, but somewhere along the way that changed, and capitalizing the year became acceptable, even conventional for wedding invitations, but it is still not any more correct than it would be to capitalize *sixth*. The year just is not capitalized in English unless it begins a sentence, and it doesn't look better that way, either. You can forgo the year altogether to save space, since common sense will inform your guests of the year anyway. You can also combine the day of the week and month with the year information in one line if your design works better that way, with no loss of formality if all the numbers are spelled out.

Saturday, the seventh of May is more traditional and formal than *Saturday, May seventh.* Whichever you choose to use, be consistent throughout your wedding suite.

The expression *half after,* rather than *half past* or *thirty* is customarily used on wedding invitations. It's more formal to use *in the morning, in the afternoon, in the evening,* or *noon,* rather than *a.m.* or *p.m.* When the abbreviations *a.m.* and *p.m.* are used (on informal invitations only), they are properly set in lower case and with periods or in SMALL CAPS, without periods.

That said, even an invitation to a black tie wedding may state the day of the month, year, and time in numerals and in a single line, when required by the typography of the design. This makes the invitation less traditional, but not necessarily less formal.

Location Lines

The name of your wedding location is usually not preceded by the word *at* unless the first line of your location begins *at the residence of,* which you will use if your wedding takes place at the home of someone other than the host(s). If the wedding takes place at the home of the host, the line should say *at home,* or *in the garden.* When a wedding or reception is held at a residence the street address is listed. Otherwise, if your site is well-known, no street address is necessary; it is enough to give the city, the city and state, or city and country in the following line. The zip code is never stated. If your wedding will be held in a specific room of a hotel or other location, you may list the name of the room in a separate line immediately above the name of the hotel or other venue.

Make sure that you confirm the accurate and complete name of the location of your wedding, including the proper spelling. You may know it as St. Stanley's, but on your invitation, the full name of *Saint Stanislaus in the Fields Episcopal Church* should appear.

GARDEN, BEACH OR SAILING VESSEL LOCATION

If your wedding will take place in a garden or meadow, on a beach, or other location which will require some consideration of footwear by the guests, you should precede the exact location with a line such as *in the garden* or *on the beach*. If your wedding will take place aboard a sailing vessel, the location of the marina or yacht club from which it will sail should be preceded by a line such as *aboard the* Elise.

Reception Line

If your reception follows your wedding at the same location, then it is always appropriate to include the reception information on the invitation.

After the wedding location lines, you should include words such as *Reception to follow, Reception immediately following the ceremony,* or *and afterward at the reception,* which is the wording most favored by traditionalists of the old school. If your reception is in a different part of the same location, you can say something like: *and afterward for cocktails on the terrace.* Likewise, when your wedding at a yacht club will be followed by a reception aboard a yacht sailing from there, your invitations could say *and afterward at the reception aboard the* Elise.

When you use a reception line beginning with *and,* there shouldn't be extra space between that line and the rest of your invitation text, since it completes a continuous sentence. If you want your reception information to be separated from the rest of the invitation text, use a line such as *Reception to follow,* which is a new sentence, and is properly separated from the location lines by extra space.

If your reception will take place at a location different from that of the wedding, and yours will be a formal wedding, you should include a separate reception card. (See RECEPTION CARDS, page 34.) It is not improper to also invite guests to your wedding reception on your wedding invitations when the events take place in different locations, just less formal. You may follow a reception line such as *Reception to follow,* with the name of the reception venue on one line, the street address (if it is not a well-known location) on the next, and the city and state (optional) on the last line.

If your wedding reception will include a meal, you should make that clear by using a reception line such as *Dinner reception to follow* or *Dinner and dancing to follow.*

You can also use less traditional reception lines such as *Feast and festivity to follow, Merriment to follow, Feasting and revelry to follow, and afterward for a picnic in the meadow,* or *Cocktails and dancing on the roof to follow.*

Attire Line

The words *Black tie* or *White tie* conventionally appear in small type in the lower right corner or in the bottom center of an invitation to a formal wedding, but only when the reception information is included on the invitation. If a separate reception card is used, it is proper to print the attire line on the reception card instead. A wedding ceremony is not a social occasion, but rather a ceremonial or religious one, and guests should wear whatever seems to them to be appropriate for that. Your reception is the social occasion to which the words *Black tie* or other designation may apply. When the reception immediately follows the ceremony, your guests may assume that the attire appropriate for the reception will not be out of place at the ceremony.

The designation of attire is offered to your guests as a courtesy, not as a dresscode. No one wants to appear inappropriately dressed at such an important social event. Unless the time and location of the reception make appropriate attire obvious, it's only fair to give some hint. Even an evening wedding at an exclusive city location should not be assumed to be a black tie event — more casual cocktail attire could well be the style. The words *Black tie invited, Cocktail attire* or *Casual picnic attire* are very informative words for wondering guests.

Black tie preferred is commonly used, but seems discourteous to some people. With those words, you offer your guests no option but to either disappoint you or show up in black tie. *Black tie invited* is a more forgiving way to offer your guests an option while expressing your preference.

The standard formal attire lines are *Black tie, Black tie invited, Black tie preferred, Black tie optional* or *White tie. Jacket and tie* is the appropriate attire line for a location such as a private club with this dress requirement. I have printed many interesting attire suggestions on wedding invitations and invitations to other wedding events such as rehearsal dinners or wedding day brunches. To be honest, I am not entirely sure what I would wear in response to some of these suggestions, but they might give you an idea for something fitting for the style of your wedding: *Resort casual; Roadhouse chic; Country casual; Attire: country picnic proper; Casual elegance; Colorful attire; Ladies are invited to wear hats; Tennis whites* (for a wedding on the courts); *Halloween attire* (for an October 31 wedding); *Guests are requested to refrain from wearing black.* The last example was printed on a separate enclosure card, and was included because the bride was wearing black, and felt that it was important that she be unique in this respect.

Response Request Line

Although it has become customary to include a reply card accompanied by an addressed and stamped return envelope, it is more traditional and perfectly correct and formal to print *R.s.v.p., Please respond,* or *Kindly reply* in the bottom left corner of your wedding invitation. This line is followed by the reply address, or, less formally, a telephone number or email address. The reply request lines may include the name of the person to whom guests should reply, if it is not the same as the name of the host.

If you are using a separate enclosure card to invite guests to your reception, your response request line is correctly placed on that card, rather than on the invitation.

R.s.v.p., the initials for the French words, *Respondez, s'il vous plait,* means *Please respond* in English, so it should not be preceded by the word *please.*

Double Wedding

An invitation to a double wedding for two sisters, hosted by their parents, invites guests *to the marriage of their daughters.* The two couples are then presented as usual, with the connecting word *and* on a line between them, and followed by the standard date, time, and location information, etc. The older daughter is traditionally presented first (even if she is only older by minutes).

Second Wedding

Second wedding invitations can be formal or informal, and may be issued by parents of the bride, both sets of parents, the couple, or grown children. As I've already mentioned, the invitations do not need to indicate the previously-married status of either the bride or the groom.

Same-Sex Wedding, Civil Union, or Commitment Ceremony

There are no special rules distinguishing invitations or announcements for same-sex weddings, civil unions, or commitment ceremonies. The invitations or announcements may be as formal or informal as the event. For examples, see the PORTFOLIO OF SAMPLES at the back of this book.

Reception Cards

The wording of the reception card follows the style of the invitation, and is in fact identical to the wording you would use if you included the reception information at the bottom of the wedding invitation. The names of the hosts are not repeated, unless they are different from the hosts named on the wedding invitation. If the location is well known, you do not need to provide the street address. A line indicating attire may be printed in the lower right hand corner, or centered at the bottom, if that's more compatible with your design.

If your invitation includes a separate reception card, that is where you should include your request for a reply, rather than on the invitation, unless you also include a separate reply card set. Likewise, an attire line should appear on a reception card if one is used, rather than on the invitation.

Ceremony Cards

If not all of those celebrating with you at your reception will attend the ceremony, then you need two cards. If you are having a large reception after a small wedding, it is appropriate that the invitation to the reception be printed on a larger card, with an invitation to the ceremony itself on a smaller enclosure card. The wording of the reception invitation is similar to that of a wedding invitation, except that it invites guests to *a reception celebrating the marriage of* two people, rather than *to the wedding* or *marriage celebration of* the couple. A reception so close to the time of the wedding is usually not *in honor of* a couple; that wording is more often used for a reception that follows weeks or months after the wedding. The hosts of the reception are not mentioned on the ceremony card. The first line of the card is usually simply *Ceremony,* followed by the date, time, and location. Ceremony cards do not include response requests or attire lines.

Mormon Weddings

A ceremony card and a larger invitation inviting guests to a reception in a home or other location is usual for Mormon weddings. An example of a Mormon wedding reception invitation and ceremony card are shown in the PORTFOLIO OF SAMPLES at the end of this book.

Enclosing Invitations to Other Wedding Events

Along with your wedding invitation, you may enclose a separate, smaller invitation to one or more events, such as a Rehearsal Dinner, Welcome Dinner, Farewell Brunch, After Party, Shabbat Dinner or Kiddush Lunch for a Jewish celebration, or following South Asian traditions, a Henna Party, Mehndhi Party or Saantek Ceremony. If you use the words *Please join us* for this additional invitation, it will be assumed that the event is hosted by the hosts of the wedding, as shown on the invitation.

Some people feel that an invitation to an event hosted by someone other than the host(s) of the wedding should not be included with the wedding invitation, but instead should be mailed separately. An example of an event like this would be a Rehearsal Dinner, traditionally hosted by the groom's parents. Others think it's fine to include an invitation with a different host. If an invitation to an event by another host accompanies the wedding invitation, a reply request with appropriate contact information may be printed in the bottom left corner or bottom center, or a request for a response for this event is included on the reply card for the wedding, with a separate line for accepting or declining. The couple, or whoever is handling replies, will then be responsible to communicate the replies to the host. An attire line may appear on an invitation to a separate event, traditionally on the bottom right corner of the card.

Activity Cards

Activity cards are enclosed with wedding invitations to invite guests to multiple events, as an alternative to including separate invitation cards for each one. The wording of activity cards may be less formal than the wording on the invitation. For example, it is usual for an activity card to list times using numerals and *a.m* or *p.m.* (or AM and PM), even if the style of the invitation is *seven to eleven in the evening*. Activity cards may have attire lines, and of course they can have different attire lines for the various events listed when that is appropriate. They can say *Please join us*, or have a title such as *Activities, Events, Schedule of Events*, or just list the events, usually starting with the day of the week and the date. I have printed activities cards that include the Rehearsal Dinner with the line, *By invitation only*, but otherwise, all the guests invited to any of the activities are invited to all of them.

Reply Cards

The reply card wording follows the style of the invitation. For example, if your invitation spells out *the fifth of May*, you will ask your guests to *Kindly* (or *Please*) *respond by the twentieth of April*, rather than *by April 20th*, which you would use if you had stated the date in that less formal manner on the invitation. Reply cards also often use *on or before* instead of *by* a certain date. The year is not mentioned on the response card.

The reply date is a question for your wedding planner, rather than for your printer, designer, or your stationer. In the past, reply dates were two weeks to a month in advance of the wedding date, depending on when the caterer or reception venue needed to know the number of expected guests. That's still the case for many weddings and receptions, but now I often see reply dates that are six to eight weeks before the wedding. When a couple is planning a destination wedding, or any wedding that includes multiple events, they may need to receive replies far sooner than would be the case if they were planning a less complicated event.

It is conventional to print a fill-in line, beginning with *M*, for a guest's name, followed by another line, *will ____ attend,* or ____ *accepts* ____ *regrets,* or *declines with regret, accepts with pleasure,* etc., set in one or more lines. There should be no space between the *M* and the line that follows it, since the *M* is supposed to be the first letter of the title of the person responding. There should, however, be a space after the line following *will* and preceding *attend,* or between the short line and *accepts* or *regrets.* Likewise, include a space after a fill-in line that is followed by a word or phrase listing a menu selection.

When some guests are invited to the ceremony only, while others will be invited to multiple events, two reply cards are printed: one version a standard simple reply card; and the other asking guests to accept or decline for each activity, in addition to their reply for the ceremony. Obviously, it is extremely important that the invitations be assembled properly, so that invitations with and without activity cards also include the correctly corresponding reply cards.

You may also simply print a reply card with the traditional lines asking for a reply by a certain date at the top or bottom of the card, leaving the rest of the card empty for a response by your guest. This can be seen as a more elegant solution, and also increases the likelihood of receiving a personal note which the couple may enjoy saving in a wedding book. This will not work for you if you need to ask for menu selections or replies for multiple events.

Reply Request Cards without Envelopes

Sometimes a response request card is included as a formal and elegant way to convey response information that might be cumbersome in the bottom left corner of an invitation. This card asks guests to *Kindly respond to* a named person by a certain date, followed by a complete mailing address in one, two, or three lines. Guests are expected to reply on their own stationery. These cards do not ask for menu selections or responses to mutiple events. A contemporary, less formal version asks for a reply by a certain date and provides an email address for the guest's response, or asks that guests reply on the wedding website (see WEBSITE CARDS, page 39). Since this card will not be returned to you, it is not accompanied by an envelope.

Number of Guests

Sometimes a short line followed by the words *number of guests* is printed on a response card because guests may otherwise not indicate how many members of a family will be attending or whether or not they will be bringing along the date you've invited by writing *and guest* on the envelope. Be wary of using this line, though, since these words may seem to invite an indefinite number of guests, even though the invitees should be obvious from the way the invitation envelope was addressed. Within the South Asian community, it is common to see a variation on this line that clarifies this issue: *Number of guests invited*, or *Number of seats reserved*, with the host writing a number on the short line following these words. This is not a query, but a statement, so it doesn't give you information about how many of the invited guests will attend, unless you add *Number of guests attending*, with a fill-in line.

Menu Selections and Responses to Multiple Events

Be careful about overburdening a small response card with menu selections or responses to more than one event, or all of this at once. It can be confusing and inelegant, and experienced caterers do not always need this information in advance. On the other hand, if it fits with the tone and design of your invitations, and it seems fun and welcoming to you to include it, go ahead. If the selections are extensive, or you are using more than one-word descriptions, and/or you are asking for responses about more than one event, you might consider using a larger size response card.

Cryptic Replies

Sometimes guests reply without actually indicating their names. You will be able to figure out the identity of the reply sender from a small number you've lightly penciled on a corner of the back of the reply card. This will be a number that corresponds to an entry on the invitation list. A reply card sent with the invitation number 29 on your invitation list will be labelled with that number, so you will know who returned it to you whether or not the sender included his or her name.

Reply Postcards

A contemporary alternative to the standard response card with envelope is the reply postcard, which must be at least 3.5" by 5" in size to be accepted by the United States Postal Service. This can be printed with the return address on the same side as the response information (you save a printing run and an envelope this way), or with the response information on one side and the return address on the other (this saves you the envelopes and some postage). One reason to do this is to save some money on printing and postage, but it's an expression of style more than anything else.

There is disagreement on the acceptability of reply postcards for formal wedding invitations. In my own opinion, it is not appropriate for an invitation to a formal wedding, but fine for a more casual one. To those who like a response postcard, it's a clean and stylish contemporary design solution; those who prefer a response card with envelope consider a postcard to be too commercial-looking and indiscreet.

Reply Envelopes

Standard invitation reply cards are returned to the host in a stamped, addressed envelope. The address printed on the front of the response envelope includes the name of the return-recipient as well as the street address, and may be set either flush left or centered. The block of type should be centered left to right on the envelope, but not centered vertically. When the stamp is placed in the upper right hand corner of the envelope, an address centered top to bottom will look too high. Depending on the size of the stamp, it will look best when the top line of type reaches no higher than the midline of the envelope.

Do not place a stamp on a reply envelope which is to be returned to you from a foreign address, and be aware that the 3.5" x 5" size reply card envelope that is standard in the United States may not be accepted by the postal service in another country. Also note that foreign guests may not be familiar with the custom of returning a provided reply card set.

Website Cards

Cards directing guests to a website created to provide information about the wedding are usually smaller than reply cards. Typically, *For more information/please visit/www.susieandmark.com* or *Please visit us at/www...* is printed in the center of the card. You can also provide more specific information about what guests will find there, with a line such as *For information about travel and accommodations/please visit...* Sometimes a reply request is included on a website card: *For more wedding information/and to reply/please visit...*

Maps and Directions Cards

The notorious problem with map cards is ugliness. It is sad to see a beautiful invitation accompanied by a clunky map. Maps downloaded from the website of your location may fit this description. If you cannot get really nice artwork for your map, perhaps created (or redrawn) in Illustrator or Photoshop, or drawn well by a calligrapher or other talented artist, don't use one. A beautiful map card with the locations of multiple wedding events can be a delightful addition to a well-designed wedding invitation suite.

Well-written directions may be easier to follow than a map, although it is hard to set a large amount of text on a small card in type large enough to be legible to someone trying to read it to the driver in a car on the way to your wedding. It is also hard to make it look good. Be as concise as possible in your wording! Don't feel that you have to give directions from north, south, east, and west. Let your guests find their own way to the town or city, and then just give them directions for the last few steps. Now most people expect their guests to be able to find directions online, but there are still cases where that isn't sufficient, for example when the wedding is near a particular grove of trees, or other feature that might not be easily located, in the countryside or in a city.

Accommodations Cards

Out of town guests will welcome information about where to stay and which airport is closest to your wedding location. An accommodations card should include all the pertinent information (address, telephone number, style, possibly $$ code for cost) for lodgings convenient to your wedding location. If you reserve blocks of rooms at special rates, your text should instruct guests to give your name or other reference when they book their rooms. Find out from the hotel how long the rooms will be held, and suggest that guests book by a date one week earlier, so that panicked guests who call you after the booking date has passed may find that they are not actually out of luck.

If observant Jewish guests will be attending your wedding from out of town, you may wish to provide information to accommodate needs for kosher meals or Shabbat lodgings within walking distance of the synagogue. Guests following other traditions may similarly require special arrangements, and an accommodations card may be a good place to provide information for them.

As with directions cards, the important thing is that the wording be clear and concise. Of course, the numbers don't need to be spelled out on an accommodations card as they will be on your invitation.

Within the Ribbon Cards and Pew Cards

If yours is a large wedding, and you'd like to make sure that relatives and close friends are able to sit near the front, you can use a ribbon to indicate reserved seating. If the ushers won't know who is to be seated in that area, you may enclose with your wedding invitations small cards printed with the words *Within the ribbon*, which your guess may present to the ushers. If you would like some guests to sit in designated pews, you may enclose small cards printed (or hand-written) simply with the words *Pew number* ____, or precede these words with *Please present this card/at St. Albert's Catholic Church/Saturday, the third of June*. You will fill in the pew number by hand.

Admission Cards

These cards are only necessary if a member of the wedding party is a celebrity or high government official, or if the location of the wedding is one frequented by sightseers. An admission card is enclosed with the invitation and personalized with the name of an invited individual or couple, and printed with the words *Please present this card/*wedding location/wedding date.

At Home Cards

When a couple is not already living together, or is moving, they may wish to inform their friends and relatives of their new address by including "at home" cards with their wedding invitations or announcements, programs, or favors. It's also a good way to let people know if a bride has changed her name, or if the couple has adopted a hyphenated name or created a new last name for their married life.

All of the information on the *at home* card should be stated in the same level of formality as the invitation or announcement which it accompanies. The new address and any other information, such as telephone number and email address(es) are listed after lines such as *At home/*bride's and groom's married names/*after the third of August.*

Other Enclosure Cards

If you would like to inform your guests of alternate plans in case of rain, or inform them of the availability of valet parking or slippers for the beach, you may communicate via small cards enclosed with your invitation as an alternative to printing additional lines on your invitation, reception card, or reply card. On these cards you may ask your guests simply to *Present this card for valet parking/on*

Saturday, the fourteenth of August / at the Horse and Buggy Club, or state that *In case of rain / the wedding will be held / at the Wonderland Pavilion / 1 Park Road* or that *Slippers will be provided / for the beach ceremon*y (guests can wear their high heels afterwards in the clubhouse for the reception).

Gift Registry Information

Although it is customary to respond to a wedding invitation with a gift for the couple, neither a wedding invitation nor a wedding announcement obligates the recipient to send a gift. Etiquette writers are adamant that gift registry information should never be printed on a wedding invitation, because including it implies the expectation of a gift. They feel that this information must only be transmitted via friends or family members, and only when asked. There's nothing wrong with establishing a gift registry, and many of your guests will be eager for its guidance in choosing a gift. They will seek out the information, so printing it on your invitation is not only impolite, but unnecessary. You can provide gift registry information on your website if you wish, but for many people, this is still thin ice.

From another perspective, just as an attire line does not dictate a dress code, but instead offers hospitable guidance to make guests more comfortable, information about gift preferences is a way of making things easier for guests, so that they can be confident that they are contributing to a couple's household in a way that is most helpful. In Hindu communities, it is customary to include *No boxed gifts* on the invitations. From their perspective, although wedding gifts are not obligatory, the practice of giving them is universal, and this information about the couple's preference is welcomed.

In Lieu of Gifts

Traditionally, guests have contributed gifts to help a couple set up a household, and when the couple's household is already established, or the marriage is merging two already established households, guests may still wish to present a gift to the couple as an expression of friendship and shared joy. Many people feel that it is not polite or correct to try to direct your friends' expressions of friendship, or to deny them the opportunity. On the other hand, no one wants to give a gift that is not used or appreciated.

A particularly gracious way to do this is to include the words, *Your presence is the only gift we desire,* perhaps on a separate enclosure card — it is less direct than *No gifts, please.* If you would like your guests to contribute to a particular charity *in lieu of gifts*, it might be better to spread this information informally by your friends and family since this suggestion implies the expectation of a gift (see *Gift Registry Information,* above).

No Children Request

There is no polite or correct way to indicate on your invitation that children are not welcome at your wedding. You may indicate on a separate enclosure card, or on your reception card, that *Childcare will be provided during the ceremony and the reception,* but not that *Mandatory childcare will be provided.* Adding *please* to *No children* doesn't make it any more polite or correct. Sometimes the words *Adult reception* are used to get the message across, but that sounds like you will be presenting X-rated entertainment.

The only courteous and correct way to make it clear that children are not invited is to send your invitations in double envelopes, and address the inner envelopes to the invited adults only. Parents who are still hoping that their children may be included will probably call to confirm your policy on this, and you'll then have an opportunity to explain that space really is limited, etc. You can include a short personal note in invitations to couples with children, saying how much you regret that you are not able to include children at your wedding, but that you look forward to getting together with Max and Lucie some other time. Whatever you do, there is a chance that some people will show up with their children anyway. I guess you could have bouncers at the door. Or you could just relax and enjoy your real-world, real-time wedding, even if the groom's mother or one of your attendants breaks into loud sobs, or an elderly relative starts coughing during your vows.

Invitation Envelopes
Return Address

It is perfectly correct to write the return address on your wedding invitation envelopes by hand, and it is equally correct, and certainly more convenient, to have it printed, particularly if you will be sending a large quantity of invitations. The return address on an invitation envelope includes the street address only. If it is printed, it is customarily set in two or three lines in the same typeface as is used for the invitation and centered on the envelope flap. You can also have your return address printed on the back (flap side) bottom of your envelope, in one line or two, or in one line on the flap of your envelope, if that is more consistent with the design of your invitation. The return address of a wedding invitation is never printed on the front face of an envelope in the upper left hand corner, despite the preference of the US Postal Service. To many eyes a return address in the upper left hand corner signals a business communication, rather than a personal one.

BLIND EMBOSSED RETURN ADDRESS

Traditional engraved invitations have been often accompanied by envelopes with the return address blind embossed, or engraved without ink. The reason given was that this way the recipient first glimpsed the gorgeous engraving on the invitation itself, and not on something so trivial as the envelope. I think it is more likely that this was recommended in consideration of the fact that early engraving inks were slow to dry, and the lettering, being raised, was vulnerable to being smeared (the same reason for shipping the invitations protected by tissues). In any case, modern engraving stands up to handling as well as any other printing, and is perfectly suitable for the return address on your envelopes. If you want to follow the tradition of a "blind" return address, you can have it blind embossed by your printer or engraver or blind stamped by your letterpress printer. If the font you've chosen for your invitation is delicate, it may not read well this way, though. In that case, you should choose a heavier style for your blind embossed or blind stamped return address. You can blind emboss the return address yourself with a hand-embosser, but it's hard to use one of those and produce a centered, straight result.

Addressing Envelopes

According to tradition, wedding invitation envelopes should always be addressed by hand, even if your handwriting is not on the level of professional calligraphy, and never addressed with adhesive labels. It's not necessary to write out house or apartment numbers, but it is better to spell out *Street* and *Avenue* and the name of the state if there's room. The apartment number should be written on a separate line.

If you are using double envelopes, the outer one is addressed to a couple or an individual, including the street address. The inner envelope is then addressed more personally, making clear precisely who is being invited. When the names of the parents, but not their children, appear on the inner envelope, it should be understood that only the parents are invited. If the inner envelope includes the words *and guest*, the recipient knows that he or she may invite another along to join the celebration. If the inner envelope is addressed to the individual only, without the words *and guest*, the recipient should know that the invitation is limited to the person to whom it is addressed. If you're using single envelopes, *and guest* may appear after the name of the addressee. The only problem with single envelopes is that even when the words *and guest* do not appear there, a recipient may nonetheless assume that he or she may invite another. The only way to be absolutely unambiguous about guests and children is to use double envelopes and address the inner envelopes in a way that clearly identifies who is invited.

Use titles as you would on wedding invitations, with full names, usually with middle names but never with middle initials, for the most formal invitations, and dropping titles and middle names for less formal ones. Married couples are listed in one line, or two if the names are long, connected by the word *and*. Unmarried couples living together are listed in two lines, not connected by *and*.

Following are the forms for addressing formal and informal single and double envelopes to individuals and couples for the most common cases. See the Appendix for forms for addressing envelopes to guests with special titles, such as clergy, elected officials and members of the military.

INDIVIDUAL
most formal

OUTER ENVELOPE

Mr. John Townsend Watkins

INNER ENVELOPE

Mr. Watkins *or* Mr. Watkins and Guest

SINGLE ENVELOPE

Mr. John Townsend Watkins *or* Mr. John Townsend Watkins and Guest

less formal

OUTER ENVELOPE

John Watkins

INNER ENVELOPE

John and Guest

SINGLE ENVELOPE

John Watkins and Guest

MARRIED COUPLE

most formal

OUTER ENVELOPE OR SINGLE ENVELOPE

Mr. and Mrs. John Townsend Watkins

or

Mr. John Townsend Watkins

and Ms. Gloria Weston Jones (on two lines since they don't fit on one)

INNER ENVELOPE

Mr. and Mrs. Watkins

or

Mr. Watkins and Ms. Jones

less formal

OUTER ENVELOPE OR SINGLE ENVELOPE

John and Gloria Watkins

or

John Watkins and Gloria Jones

INNER ENVELOPE

John and Gloria

MARRIED SAME-SEX COUPLE

The names may be listed alphabetically.

most formal

OUTER ENVELOPE OR SINGLE ENVELOPE

Mr. Alvin O'Rourke and Mr. Ricardo Suarez

or

Mr. Alvin Timothy O'Rourke

and Mr. Ricardo Felipe Suarez (on two lines since they don't fit on one)

INNER ENVELOPE

Mr. O'Rourke and Mr. Suarez

less formal

OUTER ENVELOPE OR SINGLE ENVELOPE

Alvin O'Rourke and Antonio Suarez

INNER ENVELOPE

Alvin and Antonio

UNMARRIED COUPLE
The names may be listed alphabetically, or closer friend first.

most formal

OUTER ENVELOPE OR SINGLE ENVELOPE
Ms. Gloria Weston Jones
Mr. John Townsend Watkins

INNER ENVELOPE
Ms. Jones
Mr. Watkins

less formal

OUTER ENVELOPE OR SINGLE ENVELOPE
Gloria Jones
John Watkins

INNER ENVELOPE
Gloria
John

Names on outer or single envelopes are followed by the street address.

Inviting Children

If possible, children over the age of 13 should be sent their own invitations, and over the age of 18, they should definitely receive their own. The regular protocols of addressing envelopes apply to them, just like any other individual, with most formal practice including titles and full names on outer or single envelopes.

When children are included in invitations with their parents, an outer envelope includes only the parents' names. Most writers believe it is proper to include children's first names only, with no titles, listed from the oldest to the youngest, in a line below their parent's names on formally addressed inner envelopes and single envelopes, but some feel that children's first and last names should be listed with titles below their parents' names. This can result in huge addresses on single envelopes, since the street address may follow many lines of names. Less formally addressed envelopes always include the children's first names in a line below their parents' names on single or inner envelopes.

The title *Master* may be used for a boy under the age of nine. He has no title after that until he reaches eighteen, when he receives the title of *Mr.* The title *Miss* may be used for a girl under eighteen (many would say twelve), who then may use the title of *Ms. The Misses Watkins* may be used for two young sisters, and *The Masters Watkins* for two young brothers, and *Messrs.* for older brothers at the same address. Many writers do not include titles for children even on formal invitations.

COUPLE WITH INVITED CHILDREN

most formal

> OUTER ENVELOPE

Mr. and Mrs. John Townsend Watkins

> > INNER ENVELOPE

> Mr. and Mrs. Watkins
> Serena, Jane, and Wyatt

or

> OUTER ENVELOPE

Mr. John Townsend Watkins
and Ms. Gloria Weston Jones (on two lines since they don't fit on one)

> > INNER ENVELOPE

> Mr. Watkins and Ms. Jones
> Serena, Jane, and Wyatt

> SINGLE ENVELOPE

Mr. and Mrs. John Townsend Watkins
The Misses Watkins
Master Wyatt Watkins

or

Mr. John Townsend Watkins
and Ms. Gloria Weston Jones
Serena, Jane, and Wyatt

less formal

> OUTER ENVELOPE

John and Gloria Watkins

or

John Watkins and Gloria Jones

> > INNER ENVELOPE

> John and Gloria
> Serena, Jane, and Wyatt

SINGLE ENVELOPE
John and Gloria Watkins
Serena, Jane, and Wyatt
or
John Watkins and Gloria Jones
Serena, Jane, and Wyatt

OLDER CHILDREN AT THE SAME ADDRESS
most formal
OUTER ENVELOPE OR SINGLE ENVELOPE
The Misses Watkins
 Wyatt Watkins
or
Miss Serena Watkins
Miss Jane Watkins
Wyatt Watkins
INNER ENVELOPE
Serena, Jane, and Wyatt

less formal
OUTER OR SINGLE ENVELOPE
Serena Watkins
Jane Watkins
Wyatt Watkins
or
Serena, Jane, and Wyatt Watkins
INNER ENVELOPE
Serena, Jane, and Wyatt

Names on outer or single envelopes are followed by the street address.

Wedding Announcements

Wedding announcements, which are printed ahead and then mailed by a trusted friend on the day of or day after the wedding, may be issued by the parents of the bride, both (all) sets of parents, or the couple themselves. They generally follow the format of wedding invitations, but don't list the time of the wedding, and often omit the exact location of the wedding, just naming the city, and country, if it's not the United States. Traditional formal announcements are issued either by the parents of the bride, who *have the honour of announcing,* or *the honour to announce, the marriage of their daughter,* or or by the couple themselves, who *(are delighted to) announce their marriage.*

Reception after the Wedding Date

When your wedding is small and/or far away, you, or others, may plan a later reception to celebrate with friends who didn't attend the wedding, maybe also including those who did. It's awkward to announce your wedding and invite guests to a later reception with the same card, since there are not only two occasions but also two dates to mention, which may be confusing.

Either send a separate reception invitation in addition to the announcement, or include the reception invitation as a smaller enclosure card with your announcement, similar to a reception card accompanying a wedding invitation, either printing *R.s.v.p.* in the lower left of the reception card, or including a reply card set for the reception. If you choose to include an invitation to a reception with your announcement, the reception should of course take place a reasonable amount of time from the day you send the announcements, that is, up to four or six weeks later, but not two or three months later.

You can also send an invitation to a later reception without sending an announcement. A reception invitation won't give the date of the wedding or the location, so guests won't be confused about the date and location of the event to which they are being invited.

If friends or family host the reception, it's given *in honor of* the couple, or *in honour of the recent marriage of* the couple (or *their daughter* or *their son/to*). If the couple hosts, guests are invited *to a reception celebrating our recent marriage.*

Postponing a Wedding

If you find you need to postpone your wedding, and your invitations are printed but not yet mailed, it is fine to enclose a card informing your guests that your wedding has been postponed, and giving the new date for the wedding.

If you have already mailed your invitations, you can send postponement announcements if there is still time to have them printed and mailed for arrival at least two weeks before the wedding was to take place. It is not necessary to include the reason for the postponement, but giving one will save answering a lot of questions.

Postponement announcements should be issued by the hosts of the wedding.

Chris Thatcher and Henry Robbins
announce that their wedding
has been postponed from
Saturday, the sixth of May
until
Saturday, the fourteenth of August

If you don't know the new date, time and place of your wedding, you can either recall the invitations or send a postponement announcement which does not give a new date. Recalling invitations rather than postponing the wedding is somewhat old-fashioned.

Mr. and Mrs. Jonathan Stafford
regret that
the invitations to
the wedding of their daughter
Andrea Louise
and
Mr. Martin Klein
must be recalled

A new invitation will read:

Mr. and Mrs. Jonathan Stafford
request the honour of your presence
at the wedding of their daughter
Andrea Louise
and
Mr. Martin Klein
which was postponed and will now take place
on Saturday, the sixth of September

Of course, if there is not time to mail announcements of a postponement, it is appropriate to communicate with your guests by telephone or email. If you must leave a telephone message or notify guests by email, be sure to include in your message a request for a reply indicating that the message was received. Follow up on any messages you have left or sent without receiving a response, since you really need assurance that guests won't show up for a wedding that has been postponed or cancelled.

Canceling the Wedding

If a decision has been made to not go forward with a wedding for which invitations have been sent, a printed announcement may be mailed if there is enough time to give guests ample notice to conveniently change their plans.

Mrs. and Mrs. Elmo Leonard

announce the wedding of their daughter

Imogene Alice

and

Aurelio Marco Petrini

will not take place

Programs

Programs are often worded at the same level of formality as the wedding invitations, but not always. A program may be a single card presenting the order of the service, possibly including titles and composers of the music played. A program may also be a multi-panelled folder, or a booklet, and include a listing of the wedding party, which may include relatives such as grandparents, and also the name of the officiant and the names of musicians. It may include a gracious message from the bride and groom, and explanatory information for guests who may not be familiar with the traditions expressed in the wedding celebration. Of course, the message from the bride and groom, or the story of their meeting may be in ordinary prose, and not in the special style of a wedding invitation.

When a program is a folder, the front panel usually welcomes the guests with the name of the event (*The Sacrament of Holy Matrimony/uniting*, or *The Wedding Celebration of*), the names of the bride and groom, and the date and location of the wedding. The front of a program folder can also present art, such as a drawing of the wedding location, with a "title page" presenting the information mentioned above. A more informal program, such as a small trifold, can even just have the first names of the bride and groom and the date of the wedding on the first panel, with a simple order of service, a listing of the wedding party, a message from the bride and groom, etc., on the following panels.

Place Cards

The names on place cards should be written by hand, according to the level of formality used throughout your wedding. The most formal place cards use full names and titles. It is best if the same handwriting is used for them as was used for addressing your envelopes. Try to get the names of any guests brought by your invitees for the place cards, since that's more personal than to write *Guest of Mr. Mark Cho*. Be sure to order extras to allow for mistakes and last-minute changes to the guest list. If you are using a calligrapher, don't forget to schedule his or her time in advance.

In Lieu of Favors Cards

To honor a friend or relative, or simply to regain your balance as a person and divert some of the huge expense of your wedding to something important that is not you, you may wish to make a donation *in lieu of* purchasing favors for your guests. In this case, you may also have small cards printed, with words such as, *In lieu of favors / a donation has been made to / The Canadian Cancer Society / in fond memory of Max Peters*. Or, using a slightly larger card, something like this, followed by the names of the bride and groom, and the date, on two lines:

> *In lieu of traditional wedding favors,*
> *we have made a donation to the*
> *Dana-Farber Cancer Institute's*
> *Susan F. Smith Center for Women's Cancers.*
> *Thank you for celebrating our special day with us.*
> *Katie and George*

These cards are usually arranged as part of each place setting.

Save the Date Cards

A save the date card may be as simple as a small card, with a small amount of text asking guests to save a particular date for your wedding (Please save the date/ -date- /for the wedding of Elena Jeanne Miller/and/Andrew Quinn Marcus/Bewster, New York), and ending with the words *Invitation to follow*. If yours is a destination wedding, you may also want to include travel and accommodation information, as well as any other information that might be especially helpful to your guests (*it's warm during the day, but can get very cold at night*). You can do this by including additional travel and accommodations cards, or by using a folding card. You can give your guests even more information by including a reference to a website you have set up for this purpose, but a website shouldn't be used as the only way of conveying necessary information.

Rehearsal Dinner Invitations

A traditional rehearsal dinner is hosted by the groom's parents for the wedding party, usually including immediate families of the bride and groom. The formally or informally worded invitations are issued by the hosts on handwritten notes, fill-in invitations, or custom printed or engraved invitations and sent two weeks before the event. The hosts usually *request the pleasure of your company /at a rehearsal dinner /in honor of /*(bride and groom's names). Often only first names of the couple are used. The style of a printed or engraved rehearsal dinner invitation is not expected to match the wedding invitation.

Many rehearsal dinners have expanded to include spouses and dates of the wedding party and all out of town guests, becoming a welcome dinner. In this case, guests are often invited to *a dinner honoring /*(bride and groom's names)*/on the eve of their wedding*. Sometimes these invitations are included with wedding invitations (see INVITATIONS TO WELCOME DINNERS, page 13).

Engagement Announcements and Party Invitations

Traditionally it is the parents of the bride who *announce the engagement of their daughter*. Newspaper announcements now often feature the couple, and are often written from an editorial point of view rather than as an announcement by the bride's parents. When engagement announcements are printed or engraved, they almost always take the more traditional route and are worded as formal announcements issued by the bride's parents.

Engagement party invitations are issued by friends or relatives of a couple, not by the couple themselves. The host of the party arranges for the invitations, which may be handwritten or custom printed. When the engagement is announced at a party, the invitation doesn't mention the couple; when the engagement is not a secret, the party is given *in honor of* the couple, rather than *in celebration of the engagement of* the future spouses. The invitations may be as formal or informal as the event.

Bridal Shower Invitations

Shower invitations are never issued by the couple, but rather by their friends, or relatives other than parents or siblings. Fill-in or custom-printed invitations are both used. A wedding shower is given *in honor of* a bride, groom, or couple. They are almost never formal invitations. The reply request is printed at the bottom center or bottom left of the invitation, usually a telephone number and/or email address followed by the name of the person to whom guests will be responding.

When there is a group of hosts listed at the bottom of the invitation, an asterisk by one of the names can be used to indicate whose telephone number (also asterisked) is listed with the reply request at the bottom of the card.

Thank You Notes

Thank you notes should be sent within two months after gifts are received, at the latest. They should be written to hosts of parties given in your honor the day after the event. Thank you notes should always be written by hand, on flat or folded notes, or on letter sheets.

If you choose to have thank you notes custom printed, it is fine to have joint stationery printed for after the wedding, but not for use before then. Long-established couples who already have joint stationery and won't be moving or making any title changes upon marriage may choose to ignore this rule. The only "etiquette experts" to insist that joint stationery may not be used, and that each spouse must use separate personal stationery are engravers or printers. They may have an ulterior motive. Gifts are usually addressed jointly to the couple; certainly they may also jointly express their thanks.

Thank you notes may be written on behalf of the couple by either spouse, using notes with their names as a married couple or a monogram, or on individual personalized stationery or packaged notes. It is hard to guess whether or not a couple will be sharing a last name after their wedding, and joint stationery is a good way to convey this information to friends and family. The most formal thank you notes are folding cards, with a monogram or the names, including titles, printed on the front. Less formal notes omit titles, and may be single cards rather than folders.

Notes custom printed with a message such as *Frank and Wanda thank you for your lovely wedding gift* should never be used.

Chapter Four

DESIGN AND PRINTING

DO YOU want your wedding invitations to delight your guests, impress them, dazzle them? Will your wedding stationery play a part in unifying the design of your wedding, celebrating the location or season, presenting a theme or a palette of colors to be woven throughout the ceremony and festivities? Your design decisions, including your choice of paper, typeface, printing method, illustrations and other decorations, will respond to all these questions.

A classic typeface letterpressed or engraved on fine white, cream, or ivory paper is never old-fashioned. It's timeless and beautiful. At the same time, even an invitation to the most formal wedding is not limited to that traditional style. Beyond the essentials of proper wording and form, all that is required of any formal wedding invitation is quality and elegance.

Whether you believe that less is more or that more is better, you can find or create beautiful invitations that express your taste and are true to wedding invitation form. Appropriate wedding invitation designs can be formal or informal, contemporary, traditional, merry, solemn, homey, sophisticated, understated, lavish, nostalgic, or some combination of the above. Taste is very personal, and of course, it is always informed by the fashions of the time and the community in which you live. Just like everyone's hairstyles and the bridesmaid's dresses, your invitations may look a little different to you in twenty years, but not necessarily with any loss of charm.

Paper

Let's start with the paper, because that is what invitations are made of.

The quality of your invitations will be judged in large part on the quality of the paper you use. Thicker is not necessarily better — a heavy cotton paper will likely convey quality more than a super thick cardboard laminated from lower-quality papers, but certainly a too-thin paper can make your invitations seem cheap, even with the most exquisite design and careful printing. High-quality printing or engraving will give the most elegant overall effect when you also use the highest quality paper.

There are also many good mid-quality papers in different weights, colors, and textures from which you can make beautiful wedding invitations. Be aware that not all papers will work equally well with all printing methods. Check with your printer about the suitability of any particular paper, and if you are digitally printing your own invitations, run a few samples through before buying a large amount.

Cotton or Rag Papers

Letterpress invitations are often printed on soft, thick art papers, because those best show off the textural effect of letterpress printing. The softness of these papers comes from their cotton (sometimes also linen) fiber content. Harder, more compressed card stocks made from cotton also have a different feel, or "hand," from card stocks made of wood fiber, which is what most paper is made from today. Cotton paper is also naturally acid-free, so it doesn't yellow with age. Cotton papers can be smooth or richly textured, thick or thin, with straight or deckled edges.

Like cashmere, cotton paper is more expensive, but nothing else has the same rich feel.

Handmade Paper

Most handmade papers are made chiefly of cotton. They can be smooth or very textured, very refined, or more "rustic," incorporating pressed flowers or leaves. Handmade papers are always more irregular than machine-made papers, and also cost more.

Letterpress is your best choice for printing on handmade papers. They can be marvelous for printing, or treacherous. It is just not possible to print a clean impression over an embedded twig or flower. Usually it is better to use papers with embedded materials or highly varying thickness for invitation jackets or wraps, rather than for the invitations themselves.

Deckle Edges

Paper is made from a wet pulp spread out on a screen. The deckle is the natural irregular edge of the pulp. It is on the two outer edges of paper made on a roll, and on all four edges of paper made sheet by sheet in individual molds. It can be made to be very feathery, or look more like a torn edge. In fact, the edges of paper sold as "deckle edged" are often actually torn, or diecut to look ragged.

Cards with four deckle edges paper are never exactly "square," so you can't expect the printing on them to look straight with respect to all of the sides, or be precisely centered on every card. If you use these cards, you have to understand that irregularity is part of their beauty.

Decorative Papers

At art supply or paper stores you will find dozens of special papers with beautiful and intriguing textures and patterns: marbled papers, Japanese or Thai papers with bits of foil or fibers, fine sheets with lace-like textures, etc. Some of these papers may be printed or engraved. Many more of them are better incorporated into your invitations as jackets or wraps, tissue overlays or envelope liners.

Envelopes

Envelope papers may not perfectly match the heavier papers used for invitations, but they should be compatible. It is hard for paper makers to match precisely the exact color of white or cream on different weights of papers, and color will likely vary at least a little from batch to batch of colored papers as well. Heavy art papers and handmade papers are usually not made in the lighter weights suitable for envelopes, and if they are, they're usually quite costly.

You won't find envelopes manufactured from all papers in the sizes you need for your wedding invitation, especially if you are using double envelopes, as most people do. Unless you are prepared to have envelopes custom-manufactured for your invitations, you need to plan your design with the sizes, shapes, and papers of available envelopes in mind. Most printers who specialize in printing wedding invitations will offer a selection of appropriate envelopes – at my shop, we have double envelopes manufactured (or we make them ourselves) in seven sizes and shapes, and single envelopes in five more, all in white and ivory/cream. Some printers may also stock some sizes of colored envelopes.

Either square or pointed flaps are fine for wedding invitation envelopes. Neither is more formal or informal than the other. It is usually difficult for printers to print well on the face of a pointed-flap reply envelope, and since all of the envelopes in your suite should be the same style, this is may be a reason to use square flaps. Square flap envelopes are easier to line, since it is harder to cut liners to match the shape of pointed flaps, and also square flaps lend to more design possibilities.

Printing Methods

Letterpress printing, engraving, thermography, offset ("flat") printing, and digital printing each bring a different look to a wedding invitation. There is a wide price range for each method, with the printing or engraving of additional colors adding substantially to the price. Letterpress or engraving cost more than thermography or offset printing. Digital printing can be expensive for fine art methods such as giclée, or very inexpensive. You might be able to do your own digital printing at home. Letterpress, engraving, and foil stamping presses can handle heavier papers than offset presses can. Some digital printers can print on very thick papers, but most can only handle relatively thin papers.

Letterpress and Engraving

Both letterpress and engraving are centuries-old printing methods too labor-intensive for most commercial printing today. You're not likely to find an engraved brochure or letterpress printed magazine, but the most beautiful personal stationery and invitations are still engraved or printed letterpress. Postage stamps and paper currency are examples of the virtuosity of fine engraving. Exquisite limited edition letterpress books and other pieces expertly printed on fine papers have been prized by collectors for generations. Letterpress printing and engraving are old world crafts which survive in the modern world because of the particular beauty they each bring to the *objets de papier* we value most highly. The texture they impart to paper gives it a " presence" that seems especially appropriate for wedding invitations, since they are more than notices of social events; they are part of a ceremonial occasion, and important keepsakes.

Both letterpress and engraving use a hard plate (or sometimes hand-set or machine-set metal type, in the case of letterpress), which is inked and then pressed against a piece of paper.

ENGRAVING

For engraving, the letters or design are etched into the plate and filled with ink. The paper is then pressed against the plate and pushed into the ink-filled lines. The finished product has raised lines, like fine art etching. An engraving plate is pressed hardest against the paper around the lettering or other art, smoothing out the paper there. A good engraver will eliminate this effect as much as possible, minimizing the "polish" to a small halo around the letters. You will always see impressions, called "bruises," on the back of the card or sheet, corresponding to the engraved areas on the front. This isn't a defect; it's an artifact of the process.

Engraving is unsurpassed for the exquisite printing of the finest lines, even as tiny as the ones on postage stamps you need a magnifying glass to see. Engraving inks are the most opaque, so it's the best method for printing light-colored letters on darker papers. Large solid areas or even very bold type, however, cannot be accomplished with engraving, and two-sided printing is also not possible. Relatively smooth paper is better for engraving, since the "polish" around the letters is then not so evident. The polish around the engraved areas can be unattractive on a textured stock.

High-quality engraving is always even in color and impression, and doesn't "bleed."

LETTERPRESS

In letterpress, the letters or other design to be printed are raised areas on the plate, so the opposite of what is done in engraving. When the very top surface of the plate is inked and then pressed into the paper, it leaves an ink-filled impression, without smoothing the texture of the surrounding paper. You will be able to see some "show through" of the impression on the back, but usually not enough to prevent two-sided printing.

Letterpress is very versatile, able to print fine lines (although not the almost microscopic ones of some postage stamps) as well as large solids. It can work well on smooth or textured papers. On a hard paper, the letters can have an almost carved appearance. The "bite" of letterpress printing into a soft, cottony paper will give a warmer, more embossed look.

In the finest letterpress, the printed image is crisp and sharp, uniform in color and in impression. Fine lines should be clean, with the openings of letters like *e* and *a* open and free of ink. Larger printed areas should be solid, not papery in the middle, and with clean edges. A dense layer of ink should be deposited only in the floor of the impression, leaving the walls of the indentation clean. It's the play of light on the pristine walls of crisp impressions which makes the texture of fine letterpress printing so vivid.

Letterpress printing continues to increase in popularity for wedding invitations. It's versatility inspires designers, and the texture it creates brings a feeling of warmth and authentic craft to any style invitation.

Thermography

Thermography was created as a less expensive alternative to engraving. The fresh ink of an offset ("flat") printed invitation is sprinkled with a powder which rises and fuses as it is heated. This produces raised lines, but you can tell they are not engraved because they are shiny (although matte thermographic resins have been developed), and there's no bruising on the back.

More importantly, because the thermographic powder swells as it rises, it is not possible to hold the very fine lines which are the glory of engraving. If thermography is not done well, letters might even fill in. Large solids or even very bold type do not thermograph well — the surface tends to get a mottled, bumpy texture. Thermography is never as sharp and clean as good engraving.

Some people object to thermography on principle, viewing it as a cheap and unsatisfactory imitation of engraving. I think you should forget about that, and judge thermography on its own merits. Maybe it doesn't have the elegance of fine letterpress or engraving, but it does have more presence than regular flat offset or digital printing. If your budget doesn't allow for engraving or letterpress, and you want texture in the printing on your invitations, or if you just like the look of thermography, then it's a good choice for you.

Like any other printing, thermography should be even in color and texture on each piece, and consistent from piece to piece in your invitation package.

Offset Printing

Offset printing is the "flat" printing method that produces most printed objects you encounter, from newspapers and magazines to books (including this one), brochures and business cards. It can seem ordinary, since you see it everywhere, but really good offset printing is an achievement of fine craftsmanship like any other printing. If your design depends on very large printed solids, photographs, gradations of color, an airbrush or watercolor look or other screened effect, or uses several colors, the versatility and economy of offset make it the choice for you. Most inexpensive mail order invitations have always been offset printed (although it is being displaced by digital printing for that niche), as well as more expensive invitations with complex designs, especially those with large areas of solid colors. Offset may be combined with engraving or letterpress for a mixed-media effect, but note that offset presses cannot handle the very thick papers often used for letterpress or engraving.

All the pieces of your offset-printed invitation suite should be evenly printed and match one another.

Digital Printing

Digital printing can be very inexpensive for short printing runs, such as wedding invitations, but as with other printing methods, prices and quality vary widely. Letterpress, engraving, and offset printing will print one color at a time, while digital printing creates all your colors in one printing run by depositing small dots of basic colors that blend together to create the others, so printing multicolor pieces digitally will always be cheaper than printing them by other methods. Not all colors can be matched with this process, which can be an issue if you are trying to combine digitally printed pieces with items printed by other methods. In my experience, digital printing often rubs off the printed pieces onto adjacent cards in a stack or in a stuffed invitation suite, so you may need to use tissues to protect against this. Also, depending on the machine, you may be restricted to thinner paper than you might like.

Foil Stamping, Embossing, Die Cutting

You may purchase wedding invitations which incorporate foil stamping, embossing, or die cutting from samples shown by invitation companies, or you may use any of them in your custom design. Printers and engravers who do not themselves provide these services can usually send this part of your job to another shop to get it done. In all three processes, a special die must be made. Depending on the complexity of the design, the die itself can be quite expensive.

Foil stamping uses a heated metal die to stamp a metallic or non-metallic colored foil onto your invitation. Since they are solid materials rather than liquids, foils can be more opaque than inks, but they are not always well suited for fine detail like small type, which may not break the foil cleanly, appearing clogged or ragged. Foil stamping is frequently used in border designs, monograms, or other graphics, perhaps combined with embossing. Sometimes just the bride's and groom's names, either set in type or hand-lettered by a calligrapher, are foil stamped, with the rest of the text of the invitation printed with ink, or the entire invitation may be foil stamped.

The surface of foil stamping may be matte, satin, or shiny. Shiny or even satin metallic foils are much more convincing than metallic inks, but for the same reason they can overwhelm an invitation or make it seem more like a greeting card than a wedding invitation. When used judiciously, foil stamping can create beautiful effects, but to some people, it will always be too "loud " or commercial-looking to be appropriate for a wedding invitation. It is easiest to do well on smooth stocks, but foil stamping can be especially pleasing on soft, creamy paper. The textural contrast is beautiful, and the effect is more subtle. During my decades-long printing career, I've seen foil stamping rise and fall in popularity, and rise again. But that can be said of many fashions in wedding invitation design.

Custom foil stamping will cost more than printing, but mass-produced invitations using foil stamping can be quite inexpensive to moderately expensive. Your stationer can probably show you examples of foil-stamped invitations in sample books.

Embossing presses paper between a die and a counter-die, creating a raised image which looks sculpted. Like foil stamping, it is expensive for custom work, but you can find embossed invitations in any price range. A letterpress image can also be printed without ink, or "blind stamped," giving an effect something like embossing. The black areas of your artwork will be pressed in, or debossed, and so the white areas, especially those within a black area, will appear to be raised, or embossed. For example, a couple's initials that are white, within a black rectangle or circle on your artwork, when blind stamped will appear raised within the debossed background shape. A duogram of the couple's initials or other simple art can also be blind stamped effectively, especially on a thick, soft textured paper. Since a letterpress printing plate is used rather than a special die and counter-die, letterpress blind stamping doesn't cost any more than regular letterpress printing.

Embossing is most effective on a solid white or colored paper without distracting flecks or hairs. On speckled papers, embossing is difficult to see. Simple embossing dies can be made using a photo-etching process, and these are less expensive than hand-sculpted dies. If your art needs to have a rounded appearance, or it is truly three dimensional, such as is the case with interlocking initials, an image of a family crest with a paneled or curved shield, or a view of a chapel, you will need a hand-tooled brass die, which will be quite expensive—in the hundreds of dollars. You might be able to re-use the die for thank you notes or other personal stationery.

Die cutting is like printing with a cookie cutter. Invitations with scalloped edges, imitation deckle (ragged) edges or any shape other than rectangular or square, are die cut. Very intricate die cut designs, like lace patterns, can be created using lasers. Again, it can be quite expensive to order custom die cutting, but invitations with die cuts come in every price range.

Invitation Shape

Rectangular

The most traditional wedding invitation shape is, of course, a rectangle. The usual orientation is vertical. A horizontal orientation is a less traditional, contemporary variation. The wording and the style of the design determine whether it will be perceived as any less formal than the usual vertical invitation.

Square

A square invitation can be formal or informal, depending on the design and wording. It can be tricky to get envelopes, especially double envelopes, for square invitations.

Long Rectangle

An elongated rectangle, about 4" by 9" and oriented either horizontally or vertically, is another contemporary option. These are always informal, and are sent in single #10 business-size envelopes, usually with square flaps. If the flap is at the end of the envelope, it's called a policy envelope. Policy envelopes cost more to manufacture, and they are not usually stocked by paper distributors, except sometimes in manila or kraft paper, although you may be able to find them online in other papers.

Cards cut to fit into smaller monarch size envelopes can also be used. These cards are generally around 3.75" x 7.25".

Folders

Single (two-paneled) folders usually follow the standard vertical rectangle format. Previously considered more formal than single cards, they are now considered to be equally formal, or may be even less formal, depending on the wording and design style.

THREE-PANELED FOLDER

A three-paneled folder, with all printing on one side of the paper (or both), is another less traditional possibility. One panel is the invitation, and the other panels could display reception information, or even directions or a map. The three panels could accommodate a trilingual invitation. One invitation company offers a three-paneled invitation folder, of which the third panel is the response card, which may be torn off at a perforated line and returned. This does result in the dismemberment of your invitation, but it's a clever idea. Multiple-paneled folders

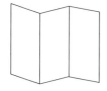

in general are more expensive than single cards, since they involve more paper and larger plates and must be scored for folding. And keep in mind that if you make these three panels too large, the trifold may be too large to fit on the smaller presses usually employed for invitation printing. It will be more expensive to print your invitation on a larger press.

GATE-FOLDED INVITATIONS

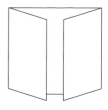

An invitation with two folding flaps, one on the left and one on the right (or top and bottom), which fold in and meet at the middle, is a gate-folded invitation. The flaps open like double doors to reveal the invitation printed in the inside middle panel. If you use a colored folder, you can glue an invitation card printed on white or cream paper onto the inside middle panel.

The two folding side panels will tend to spring open, so you will want to tie a ribbon around the folder, or seal the folder with a sticker. You can also seal it with sealing wax. Be careful with sealing wax, though. Use a flexible wax, and slide a piece of cooking parchment (or waxed paper, or foil — whatever you can easily get off of your wax afterwards) underneath the flaps to catch any wax that leaks through. You can also make your seals separately on waxed paper and then glue them on. There are also self-adhesive fake sealing wax initials made of plastic, which you can use like stickers.

Folders may be made using double thick papers, but they must be slit-scored to fold.

Rounded Corners

Rounded corners are an elegant complement to any invitation style, and a simple way to make your invitations distinctive without being fussy. With gold, silver or copper edging and a classic typeface printed in black, dark gray or sepia, rounded corners complete a soundly traditional look. Rounded corners can also add to the fresh look of a contemporary invitation design for a formal or informal wedding.

You shouldn't mix rounded and square corners in one invitation suite. If you round the corners of your invitation, you should round the corners on all the included cards. This doesn't need to extend to your thank you notes, however.

Rounded corners should not add much to the price of your invitations or the turnaround time. Now that corner rounding has become so much more popular, many invitation printers have the capability in-house.

Other Shapes

Invitation shapes departing from the rectangle or square are always less formal. It is expensive to have a special shape custom die-cut, since you will have to order a custom-made die and have your invitation run through the press again to die-cut it after printing. If you think you would like to use an unusual shape for your invitations, you should ask your stationer about what is already available from wedding invitation manufacturers.

Bound Invitation Books

The most elaborate form of an invitation is a little book, with several pages bound inside a cover, or several cards which are drilled with holes at the top or side and bound with ribbon, cord, or waxed linen thread. The couple may want to tell the story of their meeting, or simply make the invitation to their wedding more elaborate. Of course, this will be expensive if you have it professionally produced, but if you are not experienced with this kind of design and various binding techniques, that is probably the best way to go.

Type

The lettering you choose will set the tone of your invitation. Caps and small caps or all caps of a classic typeface, or a classic italic or script will have the most traditional, dignified tone. Some scripts are more lighthearted and informal. Decorative typefaces from the nineteenth century can be used to create an antique look. Whatever you choose, it should be consistent with the style of your wedding and work well with other elements of your wedding invitation design.

Each wedding invitation company offers a different selection of typefaces. It can be hard to visualize an entire invitation from one line of type, so look through the sample album to find an invitation set in the typeface you're considering. Keep in mind that some typefaces take up more horizontal space than others, so your choice may be limited by the length of the lines on your invitations (*Mr. and Mrs. Alexander Hieronymus Pastoronovich III* is very long in any case, and unmanageably long set in CAPS AND SMALL CAPS).

If you are setting the type yourself for your wedding invitations, use a graphics program such as InDesign, Illustrator, or QuarkXPress, rather than a word processing program, unless you're planning to print them digitally yourself. Files from word processing programs can't be output as the film negatives printers or engravers need to make their plates. They can be dropped into a graphics program, but the formatting will be lost. If you will be providing your text to a printer digitally, you should type the text in upper and lower case even if you would like it to be set in all caps. That way, it won't have to be retyped if you decide you actually prefer caps and small caps or some other style.

Typefaces for Wedding Invitations

If you are a graphic designer, or otherwise familiar with type, you will find that some engravers' sample books contain typefaces you have never seen. Historically, engravers worked outside the typographical tradition, using letterforms developed for engraving on silverware and other metal or glass objects. The typefaces used by printers were originally developed from the calligraphy of scribes and stone-cut roman lettering, and refined into the renaissance, baroque, neoclassical, modern, and sans serif typefaces we now use. Today, most printers and engravers make their plates from digital files, so they can use the traditional letterforms of engraving as well as the fine classic letterforms from the printing tradition, like Garamond and Bodoni, but some traditional engraving styles are still not available in digital versions, nor are some wonderful classic typefaces. For those you need to find someone who can still hand-engrave plates with a pantograph machine, or a letterpress printer who owns the metal type in question.

The following is a selection of some typefaces used for wedding invitations.

SCRIPTS AND ITALICS

Mr. and Mrs. Leonard Altshuler	LITHOGRAPHIA
Mr. and Mrs. Sanford Hornsby	BICKHAM SCRIPT
Mr. and Mrs. Elton Michaels	EDWARDIAN SCRIPT
Mr. and Mrs. Angelo Mieli	NUPTIAL SCRIPT
Mr. and Mrs. Wilson Ho	FRENCH SCRIPT
Mr. Satish and Mrs. Jasmin Gupta	POETICA

Mr. and Mrs. Leonard Altshuler HOEFLER ITALIC WITH SWASH CAPS

Mr. and Mrs. Franklin Jones GARAMOND ITALIC

Mr. and Mrs. Nigel Cooke NICOLAS COCHIN ITALIC

ROMAN TYPEFACES
Upper and Lower Case   Caps and Small Caps

Mr. and Mrs. Andrew Hall   MR. AND MRS. ANDREW HALL
MAZARIN

Mr. and Mrs. David Kator   MR. AND MRS. DAVID KATOR
REQUIEM

Mr. and Mrs. Kevin Yang   MR. AND MRS. KEVIN YANG
GARAMOND

Mr. and Mrs. Pablo Rivera   MR. AND MRS. PABLO RIVERA
BAUER BODONI

Mr. and Mrs. Raul Piperno   MR. AND MRS. RAUL PIPERNO
NICOLAS COCHIN

OPEN TYPEFACES
HOEFLER ENGRAVED
Stuyvesant

SANS SERIFS AND GOTHICS
COPPERPLATE GOTHIC
ENGRAVER'S GOTHIC
Gotham

Typographic Style

While each typeface speaks with a particular voice, the way a typeface is used can dramatically change the sense of style and formality it conveys in a wedding invitation.

Some Typefaces Are Typecast

Gotham will always look contemporary no matter what you do with it. A formal script such as Lithographia might seem to be an ironic choice for an informal beach wedding, while some decorative typefaces will just never be convincing on a formal invitation, even if they are printed in black, sepia, or dark gray on an invitation edged in gold or silver.

Type Size

There is always more space between the lines of a wedding invitation than you will see in the text of a book, magazine or newspaper, but the size of the type will vary widely, depending on personal taste and the fashion of the moment. The names of the bride and groom will be larger than the other type (or hand lettering), and the names of the host(s) and the location might also be larger than the main text, but never as large as the names of the people getting married, whose names are the highlight of the invitation. An attire line and a response line will be smaller than all of the other type, and set at the bottom of the invitation. The type on other pieces, such as a reception card or reply card, should be the same size as the text of the wedding invitation. The invitation envelope address should be the same size as the invitation text, or possibly slightly larger. Informational text on activity cards, accommodations cards, etc., will be smaller than the invitation text, but a heading on the card should probably not be smaller than the invitation text. It could be larger, although usually not larger than the names of the bride and groom on the invitation, unless that is required by the interesting design.

ALL CAPS, all lower case, Caps and Small Caps, *Italic* or **Bold**

A bold style font is not generally used for emphasis or headings on wedding invitations, since it will always be a more "commercial" looking solution than italics, all caps, caps and small caps, a larger size of the text typeface, or using another typeface entirely.

Any typeface set in all lower case will look contemporary, but whether it looks formal or informal will depend on the type size and layout, with a larger size type likely to appear less formal.

All caps, or caps and small caps, may look more formal than upper and lower case, perhaps because most ordinary text is set in upper and lower case.

Typographical Ornaments

Typographical ornaments, also called dingbats, are embellishments or flourishes like ❧, ☙, and ⚜, designed to be used decoratively with type. They can be used to separate blocks of information, such as the main invitation text and the reception information, or they can be used simply to balance your invitation design. Some typefaces come with ornaments or flourishes, and you can also buy fonts which are collections of ornaments from many sources. A type ornament can also be used as you would any small illustration in your invitation design, as a decoration at the top, for example.

Oldstyle and Modern Numerals

Typefaces come with either oldstyle numerals (1, 2, 3, 4) or modern (also called lining) numerals, (1, 2, 3, 4), or sometimes both. Oldstyle numerals are often included in "expert" fonts that may accompany "regular" fonts that come with modern numerals. Numerals do not often appear on formal wedding invitations, except in street addresses (which may be spelled out on formal invitations, but not always) or on envelopes, but they sometimes do appear in the date and time lines of less formal invitations.

Oldstyle numerals correspond to lowercase letterforms, with 1, 2, and 0 the same height as lower case letters such as *a* and *c*, and 4, 5, 7, and 9 corresponding to lower case letters with descenders, like *p* and *g*. The numerals 6 and 8 are the height of letters such as *h* and *k*, as well as all upper case letters. Oldstyle numerals fit in well with upper and lower case type, and with caps and small caps when the small caps are similar in height to the lower case letters, but they can look small next to type set in all caps, especially if you use a font such as Nicolas Cochin, where the lower case letters and oldstyle numerals are a lot smaller than the capital letters. If you are using all caps and the oldstyle numerals look too small to you, you may be able to substitute modern numerals designed for that font, or you can try setting the oldstyle numerals a little larger. If there are no modern numerals for that font, and you're not satisfied by increasing the size of the oldstyle numerals (they might look too bold), you'll need to change fonts or live with the oldstyle numerals; substituting modern numerals from another font is not an option. Likewise, if you prefer the character and elegance of oldstyle numerals, choose a font for which they are available rather than substituting numerals from another font.

Using Multiple Typefaces or Styles

For a traditional invitation, and even for most less traditional ones, you should refrain from using too many typefaces or styles. An elegant and varied typography can be created using roman, italic, and caps and small caps of just one typeface. If you'd like to use all small caps and all lower case italic for your contemporary invitation, the effect will be more pleasing if they are styles of the same typeface, rather than an italic from one font and small caps from another. If you want to use two different typefaces, they should present a strong contrast, but be compatible in weight. Good pairings might be a script with a classic roman or a sans serif, or a sans serif with a classic roman, but not two scripts, a script and an italic, two sans serifs, or two classic romans. A script with a heavy stroke is most elegantly paired with a more robust roman or sans serif, and a fine script usually looks better with another equally delicate typeface.

Multiple fonts can be used to highlight the names, or to set apart different sets of information (such as the request lines and the date, time, and location lines), or decoratively, for every other line of type, for example. If a script is used for the main text of the invitation, it is often used for the headings of accommodations cards, directions cards, or activities cards, with the informational text set in a sans serif such as Engraver's Gothic or a classic roman set in caps and small caps, since scripts are often not very legible in small sizes.

A talented and inventive designer can create festive, sophisticated invitations using a variety of typefaces, including highly decorative fonts. You might want your invitations to look like passports, or carnival posters, or just graphically impressive. You run the risk of your wedding invitations striking some as more appropriate for some other kind of party or even corporate event, but I think most people are getting pretty used to seeing a wide variety of takes on what wedding invitations can look like, and they are just glad you are getting married and inviting them.

Scripts and Italics

Alternate letters for the beginnings and endings of words, swash capital letters (*A*), and ligatures (like *ff* and *ct*) are often included with scripts and italics. Used judiciously, they can add texture and finesse.

A designation such as *II* can look strange set in a script (*II, II,* or *II,* for example). We usually substitute another typeface, such as a classic roman italic that matches the weight of the script and then tilting it to match the slope. We use Illustrator for this, but there are probably other ways to do it.

Script set in all caps is neither beautiful nor legible. Script fonts should not be set with increased spacing between the letters, since then the letters will not connect with one another as they are designed to. Scripts are usually not suitable for setting website addresses. If you choose carefully, you can find a compatible roman or sans serif typeface to set the address of your wedding website.

Maria Anderson
and
Paul Stenzler

MO SEDER

Gail Suzanne Henklein

to

Mr. Jason Brill

GAIL BRILL

Alexa Leonard
to
Mr. Seth Adam Levine

MARIA-HELENA HOKSCH

Ammiline Lucinda Belanger
and
Mr. Sebastien Henry Thatcher

LAUREN MCINTOSH

Calligraphy & Other Handwriting

You can commission a calligrapher to create original lettering for your invitation, which can be provided to your printer as original art or a digital file. Calligraphy can be very ornate and almost musical in appearance, or it can be soft-spoken and casual, but it always has a spontaneity and texture that you won't find in the uniformity of a typeface.

Most professional calligraphers can offer you a selection of lettering styles. Some calligraphers can also draw a small illustration to go with the lettering, or create a beautiful map to accompany your invitation. A calligrapher can also provide hand lettering for just the names of the bride and groom, and maybe also the name of the wedding location, to be used with type set for the other lines of the invitation. You might have a calligrapher create the complete art for all of your wedding pieces,or just the invitation, and just the letters *R.s.v.p.* for the reply card, and the words *Activities* or *Weekend Events* for the top of the activities card, and perhaps also the names of the various events with the rest of the informaion set in type.

One of the lovliest invitations I have printed was created from the exquisite penmanship of a relative of the bride. While clearly the handwriting of an individual rather than professional calligraphy, it was very beautiful, and expressed a rare warmth and dignity.

Layout

Set your type with a relatively large amount of spacing, also called leading, between the lines. This is a custom which is not only elegant, but which also connects your invitation to the ceremony itself. Just as words spoken during a wedding ceremony are delivered in a different manner and cadence than words spoken in ordinary conversation, the words of a wedding invitation are placed in a way that slows the reader down, inviting a pause at the end of each line. Because of the way the type is presented, the invitation must be read in a ceremonial manner, whether it is traditional or contemporary in style.

It is also customary and elegant to leave large margins around the text. The open space around the type is like the silence which frames the ceremony. Make your invitations larger, reduce the type size, and/or make the text more concise if your text crowds the edges of the invitation or the space within a border.

All that said, a beautiful weddinig invitation design can set the lines of type closer than is traditional, to fit in a square format for example, or perhaps because the block of type is set low, rather than centered, on the card. To succeed as an invitation to such an important event, this will need to be done carefully, though, with balance and harmony in mind.

The Traditional Model

The most traditional wedding invitation layout is also the simplest: the text is set centered on the page, with generous spacing between the lines. One typeface is used for all of the text. The couple's names are set one or two points larger than the other text. There may also be some additional space above and below the couple's names, setting them apart a little more.

You can make your invitation distinctive while keeping a traditional look by setting the couple's names in a typeface different from the one used for the rest of the text, or hand-lettered by a calligrapher. If classic typefaces such as roman caps and small caps and a formal script are used, the effect is fresh, but still traditional and formal.

A small image centered above the type might depart a little more from the strictly traditional, but still conforms to classic taste when it's done well, and it can be very charming.

Other layouts for your type are not as traditional, but they will be accepted as formal if the typography is classic and elegant, and the wording is that of a formal invitation. If your wedding celebration is not a formal event, you may nonetheless wish to design your invitation in the traditional classic style, but with a less formal style of wording.

Variations on the Centered Layout

Moving your type to the top or bottom half or very middle of your invitation, leaving an expanse of open space on the page, is an elegant contemporary variation of the centered invitation layout. To accomplish this, the text of your invitation will need to be at least a little more concentrated than it would be for the traditional layout. To preserve adequately graceful spacing between the lines, you will need to be concise in your text and adjust your line breaks so that you have fewer lines. For example, you may need to combine your request lines (*request the pleasure of your company at the marriage of their daughter*) and all of your date information into one line, and likewise with all of your location information. These lines will be long, so you'll need to choose your typeface carefully. Italics and all lower case are useful here, since they tend to be more condensed than other styles, but stay away from scripts, because they are not as legible in smaller sizes.

A layout using this approach to the type sometimes includes a small ornament or image centered at the far end of the open space above or below, to complement and balance the block of type. Ancillary information, such as an attire line or reception line, seems to anchor this style of invitation when it is centered and placed close to the bottom of the card. An attire line in the lower right hand corner or response lines in the lower left hand corner may seem to throw this kind of layout out of balance.

To be consistent, you might want to set the return address in one long line, and place it either on the back flap or near the bottom of the envelope on the flap side. If you're using relatively small type on your invitation, you might want to have it set slightly larger for the return address.

Flush Left or Flush Right Layouts

Setting your type with all of the text aligned with the left or right side of the card is a distinctive and unmistakably contemporary style. Flush left is easier to read than flush right in English. The tricky thing is to arrive at just the right placement of your type on the page with side, bottom, and top margins that feel right. This will depend largely on the length and number of lines in your text. If your lines vary too much in length, this layout may not work well for you.

Horizontal Layout

A horizontally oriented card will always look contemporary, yet it may also satisfy traditional tastes if the typography is classic and elegant. This layout presents an opportunity to combine the couple's names or other information in one especially long line for graphic effect, or simply makes it possible to gracefully and elegantly accommodate text that's too long to fit well in the standard format.

When both the bride's and the groom's parents are hosting, a horizontal format allows respective parents' names to be presented on the upper left and upper right, on the same level, rather than one set above the other, emphasizing the coming together of two families. This design is particularly suited to Hispanic heritage invitations, with each set of parents presented in two stacked lines on the upper left and upper right, with each person's full name, including surname and mother's name, on a line, the mother above the father. To work well, this layout requires the bride's and groom's names to be set together in one long line, with a connecting word, usually *and* if the invitation is set in English, or *y* if it is set in Spanish, with the request line centered above, and the rest of the text centered below (see PORTFOLIO OF SAMPLES at the back of this book).

Layouts for Square Invitations

A square invitation may be treated essentially like a rectangular one, with the type set centered, flush left, or flush right. It also offers one additional option: fitting the type into an imagined or bordered smaller square in the center of the invitation. If you have a very fortunate selection of lines to work with, you may even be able to create a left- and right-justified square of type in the middle of your square invitation, maybe even with the same number of lines above and below the couple's names. Don't try to shoehorn your text into a design like this if it really doesn't fit, though. You may just have too many lines to have an equal border of white space at the top, bottom, and sides of your invitation, or the lengths of the lines of your text might vary too greatly to create a square block of text. This may not be fatal. A square invitation can still look great with a smaller margin on the top and bottom than on the sides, and you might be able to alter your text with tactics such as leaving out the year line or including all sets of parents in a *together with their families* line, or otherwise reduce the number of lines. You can also reduce the spacing between the lines a bit to reduce the height of the text block. If none of this works, a rectangle is a better format for you.

Envelope Layout

The return address of a single or outer wedding invitation envelope is never printed in the upper left-hand corner of the front face of the envelope, but placed on the flap or even along the bottom of the flap side. A return address in the upper left hand corner of the front of the envelope signals commercial, rather than personal, correspondence.

The flap of the inner envelope (when you are using double envelopes) is usually left blank, but it can also be printed, engraved, foil stamped, or embossed with the initials of the bride and groom or other art.

Resist the temptation to center the return address of the reply envelope top to bottom. This placement won't look right once the stamp is placed in the upper right hand corner. Usually the reply envelope looks best when the baseline of the bottom line is about one inch from the bottom of the envelope or the top line is a little below the midline of the envelope.

Programs

Wedding programs may be single cards, folders, or bound booklets, large or small. A program may convey a great deal of information, which requires sensitive typography for a clear presentation. The order of service and the presentation of the wedding party might need a typographical hierarchy to separate headings such as *Entrance of the Bride* from the musical selection listed just below it, or *Grandparents of the Groom* from the names that follow below it. You should resist any temptation to use bold style lettering to bring order to the text, since you don't want your wedding program to look like a commercial brochure. It's better to follow the style you would use for an activities card enclosed with the wedding invitation, using different sizes of type or a different style or font for the headings. A script font or hand calligraphy are usually best used for the front cover of a program or headings for the order of service or wedding party presentations, with a roman or sans serif typeface if there is abundant text that must appear in a smaller size to fit.

Some programs match the design and production style of the invitation exactly, on the same paper, with the same printing method and even edging (although usually not with rounded corners), but sometimes the invitations may be expressing "understated elegance," with the programs more festive and elaborate.

Wedding programs are sometimes bound with ribbon, decorative cord, or waxed linen thread, and tied at the spine, whether or not the ribbon or thread is drawn through small holes drilled in the fold of the cover and any interior pages. Sometimes a program folder with the interior panels printed, but no separate interior pages, is decorated with a ribbon or cord as if pages were bound inside. It's important that the interior pages be slightly smaller than the cover. If they are exactly the same size as the cover, they will seem to be larger when they are nested inside.

Designing an Invitation in More Than One Language

You may wish to print your wedding invitation in more than one language, either because it is necessary for communication to all of your guests or because you wish to honor a language as an important part of your heritage. Some traditions use wedding invitations which differ widely in format from what is described in this book, and for guidance on setting up that part of your bi- or trilingual invitation you'll need to find a source knowledgeable in both the language and the customs of wedding invitations for that heritage.

One approach is to print two complete sets of invitations and enclosures, and send a complete set of single-language invitations to each guest in one language or the other. A more economical solution is to print two versions of the invitation, one in each language, on separate cards, and single-version bilingual reply cards and reception cards. Each guest receives one or both invitation cards, along with one reception card and one reply card (although you should keep in mind that European wedding invitations never include reply cards). You can also print (but not engrave) two-sided invitations and/or enclosure cards, with one language version on each side.

Folders can also be used for bilingual invitations. One option is to print a folder with one invitation version on the front right and the other on the inside right. You can also print both invitations inside the folder, one on the left and the other on the right panel, possibly with artwork and/or the bride's and groom's names and the date of the wedding printed on the front.

If one invitation is a translation of the other, rather than a completely different text and format, you can also interweave the texts, printing every other line in the second language, using a different typestyle and possibly even a second color. For example,when both languages use the roman alphabet, the text rendered in one language may be printed in small caps, with each line of text (other than the names) reprinted in a following line using the second language, set in italics. If one language does not use the roman alphabet, carefully match it with a compatible roman font, even if you do not interweave the texts. The alternating lines can also be printed in a second color.

If three languages are involved, you can print a trifold (three-paneled) card with one version of the invitation on each panel, or use three separate cards.

Most invitation companies can set type for invitations in languages other than English if the roman alphabet is used and you clearly communicate any special accents. If your text will use another alphabet, you'll need to have it set by a type-setter who specializes in that language, and give it to your printer as camera-ready art or a digital file. Another alternative is to find a calligrapher within that language community who can produce the lettering for your text by hand. In any case, it is very important that you have your invitation proof carefully checked by at least one very attentive person who is fluent in that language.

Adding Art to Your Design

Using artwork in addition to type or hand lettering is one way to make your in-vitation more personal. An image can be simply a pleasing decoration, or it can connect your invitation design more closely to you or to the event, suggesting the season or location of your wedding, perhaps presenting a motif that will be woven throughout the festivities. Couples may wish to honor their religious or cultural traditions by adding symbolic art such as a Christian cross, Islamic calligraphy, a Hindu Ganesh image, or the Chinese Double Happiness characters in their invitation design.

Illustrations

There are many ways of incorporating art into your invitation design. The simplest is to use a small illustration as a decoration above or below your text. The same image can be repeated on other pieces, such as a reception card, reply card, the flap of the inner envelope, program, menu, place card or thank you note, or you can use different versions of the same image, or different images that complement one another. You might use a cluster of grapes at the top of an invitation to a wedding at a winery, with the same decoration in a smaller size on enclosure cards. A cherry branch could decorate your invitation, with a smaller twig from the same branch on your reply card, and a different part from the same branch on your reception card. You might use a sun and moon on your invitation, with a sun on your reply card and a moon on the reception card. Or you could use completely different images, but drawn in the same style, on each piece of your invitation.

The type style should fit the style of the art you use. If your art has heavy lines it will likely look better with a typeface that is robust, and if your art is made of fine lines it may be best matched with a more delicate font.

Initials and Monograms

A monogram that won't be used until the bride's or couple's name changes should only be used on menus, place cards, and other stationery for the reception, not on the invitation itself, since it presents the couple before they are married. For the invitation and enclosure cards, you can use a design incorporating the first, or first and last, initials of the bride and the groom.

When the middle initial in a monogram is larger and flanked by two smaller initials, the center one is the initial letter of the last name. A monogram places first and middle initals on the left and right side of the larger initial of a last name. According to tradition, when a woman marries, the large middle initial is traditionally from her husband's (and now her) last name, and it is flanked by the initials of her first and maiden names. If three initials are set in a row in the same size type, they are placed in order: first, middle, last; or first, maiden, last.

Borders, Half-Borders, and Bands

A border design can be a light added touch or a rich ornamental embellishment that determines the style of your wedding stationery. An embossed or debossed panel or blind stamped border subtly frames your invitation and evokes a long-standing tradition in wedding invitation design.

You will have trouble using a border whose proportions differ from those of your invitation, unless it is made up of lines that can be extended without distortion or composed of individual ornaments that can be repeated or deleted to adjust the height or width. If the art is from an engraving or woodcut, you can't just stretch it in one dimension to make it fit your card without getting a funhouse mirror effect. You could change the proportions of your card to fit the border, but what about fitting the card into an envelope? You probably don't want to have envelopes specially made just so you can use a particular border. Using a headband or garland is not constrained in this way, and sometimes you can turn the border into a headband to make it work for you.

With any kind of border or headband you will need to fit your type into a smaller space without letting it seem crowded. You may not be able to use a particular border and also use a typeface and size that takes up too much horizontal space. Upper and lower case or italics take up less space than all caps or caps and small caps.

Background Art

You also need to give some extra thought to your type if you use a background design. Whether or not the lettering printed over your background can be read will depend on the color and complexity of the background art and the color and weight of the type or calligraphy printed over it. Even fine or small type will probably be legible printed in almost any color over a very pale and simple background design. A more vivid background will require that the overprinted type be more emphatic in weight, size, and color, or it may need to be muted a bit to allow type printed over it to read well. You can avoid the issue by using background art that leaves open spaces in which the type may be printed.

Since background art is printed in a light color, it should not be too detailed. This being the case, even photocopied art can often be used. Enlarging a small image or a detail from an old engraving or woodcut can create beautiful background art. Your silhouettes, initials, or even a map, particularly an old single-color engraved one, can also work.

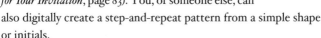

You can also use a repetitive decorative pattern, which you might be able to photocopy or scan from fabric, wallpaper, or a book of decorative patterns for artists – but not from copyrighted art (see *Finding Art for Your Invitation*, page 83). You, or someone else, can also digitally create a step-and-repeat pattern from a simple shape or initials.

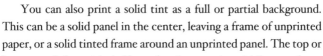

You can also print a solid tint as a full or partial background. This can be a solid panel in the center, leaving a frame of unprinted paper, or a solid tinted frame around an unprinted panel. The top or bottom or left or right half, or a band across the middle are other possibilities for this graphic treatment.

Background art cannot be engraved or thermographed, but you could have it printed offset or letterpress and then have the type letterpress printed, engraved or thermographed over it. Letterpress, offset printing, and digital printing can all accomplish both the background and the overprinting. A letterpress design with background art will have textural dimension both in the printing of the background itself and the bite of the type printed over it. A printing method that adds texture (letterpress, engraving, thermography) also adds emphasis to the type, making it easier to read.

Whenever an image comes close to the edge or bleeds over it, the invitation will have to be printed on a larger piece of paper and then trimmed to final size. This takes additional time and uses more material, so it will cost more. It is difficult to get a large area of solid ink coverage on really absorbent paper using any printing method.

Art That Works for the Printer

An image to be engraved or printed letterpress should preferably be line art, without halftones or other gradations of color. Relatively large solid areas can be printed letterpress, but not in the same printing run as small or very fine type, since the amount of ink required to get good ink coverage on the solid might flood the type. That is not a problem if your artwork is going to be printed in a different color anyway, but if you want to print your art and type in the same printing run, make sure your art is similar in weight to the type you're using. Offset (flat) printing is more forgiving in this respect, and is also a good process for reproducing halftones and other screened effects, as well as very large solids, but success will depend a great deal on the paper stock. If you have a photograph, or a watercolor image you'd like to use, it will have to be printed offset or digitally, rather than letterpressed, engraved, or thermographed (letterpress can print halftones and screened full color images, with beautiful results, but it is very labor intensive and requires a very skilled printer). Your printer can let you know if your proposed design will work well with the paper and printing method you would like to use. You should ask as early in the process as possible.

Letterpress printers and engravers will need high resolution or vector art; offset or digital printing will usually be fine with lower resolution. Check with your printer to find out their requirements before you create or scan your art.

Finding Art for Your Invitation

Look through the sample albums at your stationer, and you may well find there what you're looking for. Many wedding invitation companies allow you to mix and match or customize their designs. Many printers show a collection of artwork from which you may choose an image for them to print on your invitation, according to your instructions for size and position. If you don't find exactly what you want in their sample album, most will accept an image that you provide as a digital file or as "camera-ready" art. Digital or offset printing can use art provided at lower resolution than is necessary for high-quality letterpress printing or engraving.

A professional illustrator usually charges anywhere from $75 to $250 to draw a simple single image for use on a wedding invitation. You might have to pay more to obtain the actual artwork and permanent exclusive rights to the image. Make sure it is clear exactly what you will be buying, and how many versions you may be shown from which you may choose. Your stationer may know of a local illustrator who does this kind of work at a price within your budget.

If you or someone close to you can't draw the image you'd like to use on your invitation, and you are unable to hire an illustrator to create it for you, look through the many collections of copyright-free "clip art" available in books or on the internet (see Sources). Your stationer may have books of copyright-free art for you to peruse, or you may be able to borrow some from the library. An image from one of these sources might not be as clean and sharp as you'll need for printing on your wedding invitation. In that case, it should be reworked in a graphics program such as Photoshop or Illustrator. Sometimes the printer or engraver can do this work for you, otherwise you should turn to a graphic designer or service bureau. A stationer should be able to help you with this.

If you find an image you like in another book or magazine, or published elsewhere, such as on a greeting card, you may not use it without written permission. I have been graciously granted permission from book illustrators many times when I have asked on behalf of clients for one-time reproduction of a piece of published art on a wedding invitation. Particularly if that artist does not make a living from creating custom art for wedding invitations, he or she will probably be happy to give permission for such personal, noncommercial use. Do not try to use an image shown in an album of wedding samples by one company for an invitation printed for you by someone else, unless it turns out to be clip art. Typographical layouts or styles and color schemes are not protected by copyright laws, but original images are.

It is very important to respect copyright laws. Artists make their livings from selling their work, and a piece of art wouldn't have the same value for a client if the image could be used for free by anyone once it appears in public. According to the law, all art is copyrighted at the moment of creation, even if the artist does not formally apply for copyright protection. Statutory penalties can be high for even "innocent" violations.

Color

Few things are more expressive of personal taste than color. Colors can evoke a mood or set a tone. Color attracts attention, and can convey festivity, or a cultural identity. For example, invitations for Asian weddings have traditionally used bright colors, especially red, gold, and orange, and never black or gray, while invitations for couples following European invitations in the past used only black, sepia or dark gray. Contemporary couples choose how traditional they want to be, and today one sees Asian style invitations using black or gray, and European tradition invitations using a full range of colors.

You will make several color choices for your wedding, including color for wedding party attire, flowers, the wedding cake, favors, place cards, etc. In view of this, you might want to start out by creating a color palette for your wedding, which will coordinate all your color choices. Any color you use on your invitation would then be drawn from this palette. If you are a traditionalist, but would like to bring the fresh look of color into your invitation, you can use a colored edging or envelope lining rather than colored paper or ink.

Colored Papers

Of course, the way to bring the most color into your invitations is to use colored paper, instead of the traditional white or ivory/cream. Colored paper can have a powerful visual impact, but it also limits your printing options, and the darker or more intensely-colored the paper, the fewer the choices. The ink color you use will need to complement the paper hue, and also differ from it enough in value to read well. An ink color needs to be enough darker or lighter than the paper color to be legible. Engraving with opaque inks is really your only choice for printing light-colored type on strong-colored paper. Letterpress, offset, and thermography can work on these papers, but it's hard to predict the color outcome, since the inks are not entirely opaque, and so your perception of the printed color will be affected both by the color of the paper showing through the ink and the color of the paper around it. Really bright white lettering on colored paper is usually the opposite of what it appears: it's colored ink printed on white paper, rather than white ink printed on colored paper. The apparent color of the paper is what is printed; the letters are left unprinted and show the actual (white) paper color.

You can use a colored paper and preserve your printing options by printing your invitation on a white or cream (or other light-colored) card, and then mounting it on a larger piece of darker or more brilliantly colored paper. You can also use colored stock for an invitation jacket or folder.

If you are using a colored paper for your invitations, matching envelopes may not be available in the sizes you need or be an exact color match with the cardstock. It is expensive to have envelopes custom made in small quantities, so you should check envelope availability (for all the sizes you need) before you form a strong emotional commitment to a particular colored paper. If matching envelopes are not available, you might be able to stick with the paper you want for your invitations, but adjust your expectations to use envelopes that complement, rather than match, the paper you use for your cards.

Printing More Than One Ink Color

Many contemporary wedding invitation designs depend on using multiple colors. A border or headband design or another image is often printed in a color different from the type color on an invitation. Sometimes the couple's names are printed (or foil stamped) in a color different from the rest of the type. A decorative background design may be printed first, with your text printed over it in a contrasting color.

Unless you are using digital printing, it will always cost more to print additional colors on your invitations, since each color requires a separate plate and printing run for letterpress, engraving, or offset printing. Designs which require exact alignment of two or more colors require careful attention, and may cost more to have printed or engraved.

Wedding invitation companies may offer set designs with two or more selected colors, and will often be able to custom print one of those designs for you in your choice of colors from their palette. They may charge more for that, especially if they are printing one of the colors (background art, for example) ahead in larger quantities, and then only adding the second color (your text in this case) to order. For an extra charge, many will allow you to choose a special PMS color not shown on their ink color chart.

Regardless of how many colors are involved and what printing method is used, the colors should be uniformly printed on all your pieces, although keep in mind that ink colors may look slightly different on different papers, even if the papers are the same color. One paper may absorb ink differently than the other.

Don't forget about embossing or blind stamping as a second color. The effect is similar but more subtle than printing a second color. A design that might be overpowering if printed in a color can be very elegant when blind stamped or embossed.

Edgings

Some printers and engravers offer a kind of edging on invitations that follows the traditional practice of applying gold leaf to create the gilt edges sometimes found on the pages of books, such as Bibles. An edging is hand-applied to the four side surfaces of a stack of invitations, as it would be to the three sides of the block of pages of a closed book. When the stack is separated into individual cards, each has a coating of gold, silver, copper, or another color, metallic or non-metallic, on the four outer edges, but not on the front or back surface. If the stack is tilted at a slight angle and sanded before the edging is applied, a beveled surface is created on each card, and the edging will appear partly on the front surface of the card along each edge as well. Only a relatively hard, smooth paper can be sanded to create a bevelled edge.

Two kinds of edging are available for your wedding invitations: foil edgings and painted edgings. Foils used for edgings are available in dozens of colors, but you won't necessarily find an exact match for every printing ink. Spray paint, which is what is used for "edge painting," or "hand-painted edges," on the other hand, may be found to match almost any non-metallic ink color. Foil colors can be shiny or matte, and will have a more enamel-like surface than spray paint, and since a solid material is applied to the edge of your invitation when foil is used, it will never bleed into the card. Gold, silver or copper spray paint, like those printing inks, will convey the color, but don't expect paint or ink to look shiny and metallic like gold, silver or copper foil, any more than printed or engraved gold ink will look like gold foil stamping. But if you really need a particular color not available in foil, painted edges will be the best choice for you.

Edging creates a relatively subtle, but striking effect, even on regular weight papers. Sky blue edging beautifully completes an invitation printed in matching sky blue ink on bright white paper. A bright edging color like orange or magenta won't overwhelm your invitation, even on double thick papers, but its fresh presence will not be missed. Edging your invitations is a great way to bring in a color accent that will be woven throughout the design of your wedding, whether or not it's the color you choose for your type.

Sometimes all the pieces of a wedding invitation suite will be edged, but it's perfectly acceptable to edge only the invitation, or the invitation and the reception card, but not the reply card. This is in contrast to corner rounding, which should be done for all the cards or none of them.

Adding an edging usually costs less than adding a second printed color. Depending on whether your printer handles edging in-house or sends your invitations out to another business to be edged, adding edging to your cards may add weeks to the turnaround time or not affect it at all.

Envelope Linings

The open flap of an envelope presents a large surface area you can exploit for displaying color, pattern, or texture to your invitation recipient. You can line your envelopes with a tissue or paper in a color that matches or complements another color used on your invitation, or it can bring several colors together in a decorative pattern. An envelope lining can also bring a new textural note into your invitation design. It just has to be thin enough to allow your envelope to fold well and permit the invitation to slide easily in and out (the invitations might need to be trimmed a bit to fit in an envelope with a thick liner). Usually only inner, ungummed envelopes are lined, because the recipient might not see much of an envelope lining installed in an outer or single envelope, particularly if they use a letter opener.

A real envelope lining is a tissue glued to the envelope paper before it's folded and glued into an envelope. Very few envelopes are manufactured this way, and you don't get to choose the lining paper. To get a similar effect, a paper can be cut to the right size and shape, and glued to the inside of the flap, extending down into the envelope. Most national stationery companies offer this kind of envelope lining for your wedding invitations. You can choose from their selection of papers or possibly send them another paper you'd like to use. Your stationer may offer this service as part of your complete wedding invitation package. You can also line your envelopes yourself, following the directions given on pages 126-128 in APPENDIX B.

Although they are beautiful, tissue envelope liners do have a drawback: they tend to pull out of the envelope with the invitation. At my shop, we glue a glassine hinge attaching the tissue liner to the envelope, so that the tissue can move up and down as the flap opens and closes, as it must, but stays attached to the envelope so that it won't pull out with the invitation. This is labor intensive, but usually effective.

Addressing Envelopes

Hand Calligraphy

To find a calligrapher to address your envelopes, ask your stationer or wedding planner, or contact the Society of Scribes (see Sources). Ask for examples of the styles from which you may choose, and not just one-line samples but entire invitations. If you would like your envelopes addressed in a color other than black, confirm that your calligrapher is able to do this. If you will be using lined envelopes, inquire about possible additional charges for addressing them. Your invitation list should be typed rather than handwritten; your envelopes will be addressed exactly as the list is typed. Some calligraphers will check zip codes and correct your lapses in addressing etiquette, but don't assume that these services will be provided. It is not inappropriate to ask for references. Good questions to ask would be about the quality, consistency, and timeliness of the calligrapher's work.

Machine Calligraphy

Some stationers offer machine calligraphy for addressing your envelopes and even as a printing option for your wedding invitations. This mechanical process will never look like the handwork of a calligrapher, and to some it is too impersonal to be acceptable. But if you really do not have the penmanship to address your invitations or the budget to hire a calligrapher, and can't find a willing friend or relative with nice handwriting to help, you may want to look into this option. Check with your stationer for price and turnaround time.

Tissues, Jackets & Wraps, Ribbons, and Other Embellishments
Tissues
Inspired by the custom of including tissues with engraved invitations, some invitation designs incorporate a vellum, glassine, rice paper, or tissue overlay, either as a decorative element or printed with the text of the invitation, and placed floating or mounted over a decorative paper or a card with a printed background. This style was very popular during the 1990's, with a vellum sheet printed with the invitation text attached to a decorative backing paper, with a ribbon drawn through drilled holes and tied in a bow at the top.

While they can work well with engraving, offset, or digital printing, vellum and glassine are not great papers for letterpress printing, and tissue is very hard to feed through our presses, so at my shop, we generally use rice paper when translucence is called for. I've printed lovely invitations that included lines of poetry or sacred words printed on rice paper and placed over the invitation.

Wraps
Sometimes a tissue or another paper folds entirely around the invitation, becoming a wrap. A wrap can be simply folded to enclose an invitation, or be tied with a ribbon or cord. Some designers offer wraps with their invitations, and you can also make them yourself. Japanese and other Asian papers, for example, come in many beautiful textural patterns, and fold easily enough to be used as wraps, but other papers may need to be scored to fold around the invitation. (A score is a line printed by letterpress, but without ink, so just leaving an impression along which the paper will fold more easily.)

Jackets and Boxes
The next step in complexity is a jacket or pocket folder, made to hold the invitation or the invitation and all the enclosure cards. A jacket can be bound together by a ribbon, cord, or paper band, sealed with a sticker or with sealing wax. Your stationer probably carries some styles which use jackets, wraps or folders, or even boxes to enclose wedding invitations. You can also customize simple invitation

designs with jackets, folders or wraps that you make yourself or buy through your stationer or online.

This is also an area in which a professional wedding invitation designer may excel. When you get beyond folding paper to using fabrics and other materials, bookbinding skills come into play. The beauty of fine materials can be fatally compromised by poor craftsmanship. If you want to do something really stunning, using very fine or unusual materials, you should probably consult a professional.

Ribbon, Decorative Cord, and Waxed Linen Thread

A ribbon can be used functionally — to bind a jacket or wrap or otherwise hold the elements of a wedding invitation together — or it can be used purely decoratively. Some invitations have holes drilled, so that a ribbon can be threaded through and then tied into a bow to adorn the card. If a ribbon, cord or waxed linen thread is used to hold together the elements of your invitation, it can also be used to attach a tag. A decoration such as a dried flower can be slipped under a ribbon or cord to embellish your invitation.

Paper Band

A paper band with ends glued, or sealed with a sticker or sealing wax, can wrap around an invitation as a decorative element. It can also keep a jacket or wrap closed as a sticker or ribbon would. The paper band may be printed, or made of a decorative paper.

Assembling Invitation Sets

The front of your invitation should face the recipient as it is removed from the envelope, with the right-hand side of the card or folder closest to the flap. If you are using tissues, they should be placed directly on top of each card to which they correspond. Enclosure cards should be placed face up on top of the invitation in order of size, with the largest card on the bottom. The reply card is placed under the flap if its envelope, with the lettering facing up.

If you are using double envelopes, the inner envelope containing the invitation and enclosures goes in the larger outer envelope with the unsealed flap at the top but facing away from the recipient. When the outer envelope is opened, the names on the front of the inner envelope face the recipient.

Mailing Jacketed, Wrapped or Boxed Invitations

If you are using a jacket or wrap for your invitation, it may enclose only the invitation, or it may hold all of the enclosure cards as well. If only the invitation itself is enclosed and bound with a ribbon, the enclosure cards may be slipped under the ribbon on the back, face up in order of size, with the largest card on the bottom. Either way, the jacketed or wrapped invitation will be enclosed in an envelope for mailing.

If you use a single outer envelope over the jacket or wrap, you may address it as you would any single envelope, or you may use it like a conventional outer envelope and address the jacketed or wrapped invitation package as if it were an inner envelope. You may be able to write the names of invited guests directly on the jacket or wrap, or on special labels, or if you are tying the package with a ribbon or cord, you can attach a tag inscribed with your guests' names.

If you do want to use double envelopes in addition to your wrapped or jacketed invitation package, make sure that the sizes you'll need are available in the paper you want to use.

A clear mylar or plastic envelope may be used to enclose an invitation with a jacket or wrap or even one in a box. Usually the address and return address are inside the package, mounted on a label on the box, jacket or wrap, or otherwise positioned to be read through the clear envelope. A mailing label can also be affixed to the clear envelope. Personally, I was skeptical of mailing a wrapped, jacketed or boxed invitation in a mylar or plastic envelope, and have always recommended a more sturdy mailer, but custom wedding invitation designers have assured me that this works. I guess mylar and plastic are tough, even though they are thin, and they tell me people do not seem to feel that the presentation of the invitation is cheapened by the clear envelope.

Sealing Envelopes

Never use an automatic envelope-sealing machine for your invitation envelopes. It may be difficult to feed your assembled invitations through the machine, and the manner and position of the moisture application for sealing might not be correct. Compared to regular business envelopes, the heavier, and often textured, stocks used for wedding invitation envelopes may need more pressure to ensure a seal. Make sure all of your envelopes have been sealed before you mail them! I recommend that you use a glue stick to seal lined envelopes, since applying moisture to the flap adhesive might cause the liner paper to cockle, or its color to bleed. A glue stick may be easier to use and more reliable for sealing any envelope.

Postage for invitations

After you have weighed a complete assembled and stuffed wedding invitation and determined the proper postage, choose nice stamps from those available at your post office, or have some printed by an online vendor, using art that you provide. The postage for your invitation will probably be more than the amount needed on your reply card envelope, so you likely won't be able to use the same stamps for both, but you might be able to find something that has an image or colors that you particularly like and maybe even coordinates with your invitation design. You can even use vintage stamps. Consider asking that your invitations be hand-cancelled, so that postal barcodes will not be printed along the bottom, but you will need extra postage for that. You might need to pay for extra postage and get hand-cancelling anyway, depending on the size, shape, and thickness (the USPS sees that as "rigidity") of your invitation.

Chapter Five

Proofs

Always order proofs of your wedding invitations, and check them carefully. A proof is a printout of your invitation text, made from the digital file before the plate is made, and faxed or emailed to you. It won't be a sample invitation, printed or engraved on the stock you've chosen, because that would entail the making of a plate and all the setup necessary to actually print or engrave all your invitations. That kind of proof is called a press proof, and costs a lot more, if it's available at all. If there is an extra charge for a regular proof, it will be very small relative to your whole expenditure, and worth it whatever the price. The proof is your last opportunity to catch any errors in the text, originating either in the copy you submitted or in mistakes by the typesetter, before the plate is made. Print your proofs out and have all the important people involved look at them. Do not just look at the proofs in miniature on your phone! If you sign off on the proofs and there does turn out to be a mistake, you'll either have to live with it or pay to have your invitations reprinted. No one wants that to happen, and you're in the best position to make sure it doesn't.

Not all wedding invitation companies charge for a change in the text if it's your mistake or for another reason, but some charge a lot. Before you submit your copy, check everything carefully, especially all proper names, such as the spelling of your future spouse's rarely used middle name. Make sure everything is there and correct: date (right date for that day of the week!), time, place. And don't forget that a proof is for more than catching typos. After seeing the proof, you might want to make some changes in the size or spacing or style of the type, and it's better to pay a little to do that now than to later really wish you'd changed it.

Proof Checklist

Go down this list before you submit your text and also after the proof is returned to you by the printer. It is easy to miss errors when you are very familiar with the text, so ask a friend or family member to make an additional check of the printer's proof for you before you sign off on it.

1. Check all spelling for correctness.

2. Check proper names again, including the name of the location.

3. Check street numbers and zip codes again on both the invitation envelope and the reply envelope. If you have given your mother's address for the reply envelopes, make sure you did not inadvertently complete it with *your* zip code.

4. Make sure the date, time, year, and all the location lines are correct.

5. Make sure the day of the week corresponds to the date.

6. Make sure no word spaces have been omitted or doubled.

Where to Buy Wedding Invitations

It was not long ago that the selection offered by wedding invitation companies was very limited, and wedding invitation designs hardly changed from year to year. All that has changed now, and a very wide variety of styles and qualities are available. With the advent of new technologies, it's now easy to work with an artisan who doesn't live in your local community. What would have been available to you ten or even five years ago only by working with a graphic designer, you can buy from your local stationer today.

Wedding magazines show more stationery than they did in the past, and looking through them is a good place to start gathering information. Keep in mind that many, if not most, of the stunning examples of invitations shown in wedding magazines and coffee-table books, not to mention online postings, are custom invitations which may be outside your budget or take more time than you have available. Still, they'll show you the latest styles and possibly give you an idea of what you would like to pursue for your own invitations.

When it comes down to actually purchasing your invitations there are issues like price, turnaround time, quality, and reliability that make a big difference in which source you should choose. If you are attracted to a particular design, but find that it is far outside your budget, the turnaround time is three weeks too long, or your stationer hates to deal with that company because they make so many mistakes, produce work that is uneven in quality, and/or are often late to deliver, don't lose heart. You will likely be able to work with your stationer to get the look and feel you want with something that you can afford from a company your stationer has confidence in.

Your Local Stationer

For the best assistance with all aspects of this essential experience in your progress toward the actual exchange of vows, you should turn to a knowledgeable stationer. A knowledgable stationer will guide you through the entire process of planning, selecting or designing, and then ordering your invitations. They will then be your liaison with the small to enormous company which will be producing your order. They will check to make sure you didn't leave out the time or date of your wedding, help you decide how many to order of which item. There is a lot to choose from and so many big and little decisions to be made. It is best to have the benefit of a person you can meet with face to face, who will help you make sure you really have covered all the bases and who will stand behind the finished product.

Some stationers work entirely by appointment, but most will consult with you on a drop-in basis. When you do meet with them, you will be shown albums and loose samples showing typefaces, ink colors, and designs offered by several purveyors of wedding invitations. Some stationery stores have just about every album in existence; others carry a select number which they consider to be the highest quality and the most reliable, and the most appealing for the clientele they serve. They will help you choose from the many options, taking into account your budget and taste as well as your time frame. Most wedding invitation manufacturers allow at least some flexibility so you can work with your stationer to create a truly distinctive custom invitation using the albums they have at hand.

Turnaround times vary from days to weeks, with the average probably being two weeks and two or three months the longest you will have to wait. This does not include the time you spend making your selections, or any time spent going back and forth with proofs, which can add substantially to the overall time it takes to get your wedding invitations, so get started as soon as you have the date, time, and place established.

Expect to pay in full, or at least a 50% deposit, when you place your custom order with a stationer.

EXTRA SERVICES PROVIDED BY SOME STATIONERS

Some stationers have calligraphers on staff, or can refer you to a calligrapher to address your envelopes or produce the hand-lettering for your printed or engraved invitation text. They may also be able to address your envelopes with mechanically-produced calligraphy (see also ADDRESSING ENVELOPES page 44).

Lining envelopes, assembling invitation sets, including those involving the tying of many identical bows, may be services offered by your stationer.

"IMPRINTABLES"

"Imprintable" invitations are offered by many, but not all, stationers (they are also available over the internet or by mail order). These are boxed invitations printed with a design, leaving a space for your text to be digitally printed. They may involve vellum overlays, wraps, die-cuts or pre-drilled holes through which you'll thread ribbons and then tie bows. The simpler, smaller ones cost about $1 to $2 each. Reply card sets run about $.75 to $1.50. You can digitally print these yourself, but if your stationer offers the option of doing that for you, you should consider doing that. It can be very frustrating setting up the correct layout and getting the cards to feed properly. Also, some digital printers deposit ink which may rub off or smear easily. Imprintables aren't nearly so economical when you've had to buy extra boxes to make up for mistakes in printing. You should count on a minimum of 10% to 20% extra to allow for spoilage. Ask your stationer if they offer dgital printing and about their prices and turnaround time before you buy imprintables.

HAVING YOUR INVITATIONS SHIPPED DIRECTLY FROM THE MANUFACTURER

If you're ordering through a stationer, I recommend that you don't have your wedding stationery sent directly to you or a calligrapher from the manufacturer. As your liaison with the company making your invitations, your stationer should fully inspect your order before you pick it up. He or she should confirm that everything, including the quantity of each item, is precisely what you ordered, and rectify it with the manufacturer immediately if it's not.

Graphic Designer or Custom Wedding Invitation Designer

If you don't want to choose or customize your invitations from a sample album at your local stationer or from the offerings displayed by online vendors, you can commission a graphic designer to create an original design for you, although you should be aware that most graphic designers are not familiar with all the particularities of wedding invitations any more than most other people are. While providing a distinctive design for you, a graphic designer whose business is based on corporate design work might not realize that most wedding invitations are mailed in double envelopes, or be able to help you out with the wording of your invitations. Inner and outer envelopes, and even small reply envelopes are not always readily available to the local printers used by graphic designers for their usual commercial printing jobs, and having them specially manufactured is expensive. Also be aware of how much work it is to design all the items of a wedding invitation set — invitations and envelopes, response card sets, with perhaps also reception cards, directions cards and/or maps, and thank you notes. It can be an expensive job and a tall favor to ask of a designer friend.

Designers specializing in custom wedding invitations have usually done their homework on etiquette and the conventions of wedding invitations. They have spent time locating sources of paper, envelopes, fabrics, ribbons, and other special materials, while developing working relationships with printers and engravers. Some of them specialize in dazzling presentations, like gorgeous fabric- covered jackets or boxes. They will want to work closely with you to get ideas for a design that uniquely expresses your taste and succeeds as a striking introduction to your wedding. You should be prepared to spend some time reviewing selections of materials and design options. This kind of work can be very expensive, so it will make the most sense for you if your invitations are near the top of your budget priorities.

You may be able to find a custom wedding invitation designer through your event planner. Wedding magazines and books often show the work of custom designers and also list their contact information.

Some calligraphers offer the complete services of a custom invitation designer, designing and hand-lettering all the pieces of your wedding stationery and then handling printing or engraving, and possibly the assembly of your invitations for you as well. Some calligraphers are also accomplished artists able to draw an image to accompany the text, or a beautiful map in the same style as the lettering of the other items in your invitation set.

Working with a graphic designer or custom wedding invitation designer is almost certainly a more time-consuming option, and, unless the designer is your sibling or friend, the most expensive.

A Local Printer or Engraver

With or without the services of a graphic designer, you may turn to a local printer or engraver for your wedding invitations. Your local printer/engraver may in some cases be able to design your invitation as well as produce it, but more likely you will need to provide digital files or camera-ready art which you (or your designer) have created, and choose from the paper and envelopes your printer can obtain. You may be able to provide paper and envelopes, with extras for setup. Your printer or engraver may also direct you to a catalog, from which your wedding stationery will be ordered rather than printed on site. In any case, be sure to look at samples of a printer's or engraver's work and get a clear commitment to a price and time frame before you proceed. Expect to pay a 50% deposit when you place your order.

LETTERPRESS: HANDSET AND MACHINE-SET TYPE OR PLATES

Most letterpress printers now use photopolymer plates, which are made using negatives generated from digital files or camera-ready art. You will have a digital printout proof to check before the plate is made.

Some local printers still use handset type or machine-set metal type such as Monotype or Linotype, which are set according to your instructions. A proof is printed from the type after it has been set. It is a lot harder and more expensive to make changes in metal type than in a digital file, and there are technical obstacles to adjustments in letterspacing that you don't encounter digitally. When metal type is used, accompanying images are printed from magnesium, zinc, or copper photoengravings mounted on wood, and it is difficult to incorporate this kind of artwork into the same print run with metal type and get good results from both.

I began my letterpress printing career with metal type and wood-mounted metal photoengravings over thirty-five years ago, and I still love them. But the truth is, photopolymer plates give as good or better results, and working with digital files is far more flexible and timely. Metal type wears out, and printers today can't replace it as printers in the past were able to replace theirs. Linotype or Monotype are set and cast by machine from softer metal than foundry type, and they can wear out even in the course of one small job. Printers using Linotype in particular are usually reluctant to put enough pressure on the type to get a crisp impression, knowing that if they do so, Bodoni Book might look like Bodoni Bold by the end of the run. The kind of paper used for raffle tickets doesn't need much impression to transfer the ink (and the aesthetic requirements for raffle tickets aren't especially high, either), but an art paper or any other stock you'd probably want to use for your invitation will need quite a bit of pressure on the type to overcome the surface of the paper and leave a crisp impression. Printers using handset type are also often reluctant to put enough impression on their irreplaceable type, because that, of course, is how it wears out.

The point is, you may not get the results you expect from the local letterpress printer of raffle tickets, or for that matter, an offset printer who is willing to ink up the old letterpress in the back that either hasn't been used for years, or only for numbering, scoring, or die-cutting. Make sure you look at samples, and make sure you clearly communicate to your local shop what it is you're looking for.

DIGITAL ENGRAVING OR HAND ENGRAVING

All the national wedding invitation companies and most other engravers now use photoengraved plates made from digitally produced negatives. This has the same advantage for engraving that it has for letterpress: it is more flexible and the customer can get a proof quickly, before the plate is made. Still, more expensive engraving plates made by hand, freehand or with the aid of a pantograph machine, do offer results superior in some ways to photoengraved plates. A finer, deeper line can be engraved by hand, and fine lines are the glory of engraving. The exquisite detail of a monogram, coat of arms, or other intricate image designed and engraved by hand can't be duplicated by any other process. Engraving from a photoengraved plate made from artwork drawn with a pen will never have the same line quality or level of detail as engraving from a plate with lines cut by hand directly in the metal.

If you plan to have your invitations engraved and have a fine enough eye to appreciate the difference between pantograph or hand engraving and digital engraving, you should seek out one of the few shops that can still do this for you. You will need to be willing to choose from the scripts and other typefaces for which that particular engraver has patterns and also allow a little more time for the production of your invitations, which will be more expensive than if they were produced digitally. Some of the national companies can still provide pantograph engraving, even though it's no longer shown in their catalogs. Ask your stationer about this.

Over the Internet or by Mail Order

Ordering your invitations by mail or over the internet is another option, and obviously one that omits the personal contact and service offered by a stationer or designer as well as the security of doing business with a known local entity. Mail-order invitations are generally on the low end of price and quality; internet offerings run the gamut. There are internet businesses that are essentially online stationery stores, offering the products of many different vendors. Some businesses sell online exclusively. If you do choose to order by mail or online, make sure you get samples, and are sure of the manufacturer's reliability with respect to quality, turnaround time, and remedy in case the order you receive is not what you expected. Keep in mind that it is very difficult to asses quality from an onscreen image or description alone. Expect to pay in full when you place your order.

In any case, if you have taken advantage of the advice and experience of a stationer in planning your wedding invitation, don't then place your order with an internet vendor. The service stationers provide is their livelihood. They pay rent so that you may sit in a local store, seeing and touching real samples from a variety of suppliers as you make your decisions. The stationery store is one of the last traditional businesses where they actually sell what they say they do, offering good old-fashioned personal service to a local community. If you have used their services, you need them, and by purchasing your invitations there you will be doing your part to make sure they're still there when you need them again.

A *P*ORTFOLIO OF SAMPLES

All examples are reduced in size from the originals.
All illustrations copyrighted by the artists.

MR. AND MRS. ROBERT DREWE

REQUEST THE HONOUR OF YOUR PRESENCE

AT THE MARRIAGE OF THEIR DAUGHTER

Catherine Elizabeth

TO

Mark William Smith

SATURDAY, THE SEVENTH OF NOVEMBER

TWO THOUSAND TWENTY

AT FOUR O'CLOCK IN THE AFTERNOON

THE CHAPEL OF THE NATIVITY

GRACE CATHEDRAL

SAN FRANCISCO, CALIFORNIA

Traditional Formal Wedding Invitation The calligraphic names (by Maria Helena Hoksch) are beautifully printed in the same color as the type, or they could be printed in another color, or foil stamped.

DINNER AND RECEPTION

IMMEDIATELY FOLLOWING THE CEREMONY

THE MARK HOPKINS HOTEL

SAN FRANCISCO

VALET PARKING   BLACK TIE

Traditional Formal Reply Card and Reception Card The attire line is properly on the reception card, rather than the invitation.

KINDLY REPLY BY THE FIFTEENTH OF OCTOBER

M_____

_____ ACCEPTS   _____ REGRETS

Mr. and Mrs. Anthony Jumonville

request the honour of your presence

at the Nuptial Mass uniting their daughter

Antoinette Grace

and

Mr. James Raymond Gillis

in the Sacrament of Holy Matrimony

Saturday, the ninth of March

two thousand twenty

at six o'clock in the evening

Holy Name of Jesus Church

New Orleans, Louisiana

Roman Catholic Wedding This traditional invitation suite is for a Roman Catholic wedding celebrated as a Nuptial Mass.

Dinner reception

immediately following the ceremony

La Salle's

Valet parking

Traditional Formal Reception Card Plus Website Card The inclusion of a website card is a contemporary addition that makes the wedding invitation no less formal or traditional in style.

For information about

accommodations in New Orleans

please visit our wedding website

www.toniandjames.com

ב"ה

DR. DAVID REYNOLDS

TOGETHER WITH

MR. AND MRS. ALBERT GRIFFIN

REQUEST THE PLEASURE OF YOUR COMPANY

AT THE MARRIAGE OF THEIR CHILDREN

hannah cecile reynolds

AND

jerome alex griffin

SUNDAY, THE TWENTY-SEVENTH OF JUNE

TWO THOUSAND TWENTY

CEREMONY AT SIX O'CLOCK IN THE EVENING

MUSEUM OF FINE ARTS

BOSTON, MASSACHUSETTS

BLACK TIE

Non-traditional Formal Wedding
From the *bet hay* in the upper right hand corner, you know that this will be a religious ceremony, but since the location is not a place of worship, the hosts request *the pleasure of your company*, rather than *the honor of your presence*. Centering the attire line at the bottom is less traditional than placing it in the bottom right, but does not take away from the formality of this contemporary design.

FOR INFORMATION ABOUT

ACCOMMODATIONS

AND ALL WEDDING DETAILS

PLEASE VISIT:

HANNAHANDJEROME2O2O.COM

Mr. and Mrs Michael Jonas Workman

request the pleasure of your company

at a wedding celebration for their daughter

Meghan Amy

and

Henry Patterson Young

son of Mr. and Mrs. Timothy Clarke Young

Saturday, December nineteenth

two thousand twenty

from half after six until ten o'clock

Salt Lake Country Club

Salt Lake City, Utah

Morman Wedding Whenever more guests will be invited to the reception than will be present at the ceremony, a ceremony card for guests who will attend both is enclosed with a larger invitation.

Temple Ceremony

Saturday, December nineteenth

at half after one o'clock

Salt Lake City Temple

MARIA CECILIA SUAREZ DE MILLARES
CESAR ANTONIO MILLARES MENDIZABAL

BEATRIZ FERNÁNDEZ DE GUILLARTE
LUIS ALBERTO GUILLARTE MOREIRA

TIENEN EL PLACER DE INVITARLE (S) AL MATRIMONIO DE SUS HIJOS

Natalia Maria y Javier Eduardo

QUE SE CELEBRARÁ

EL SÁBADO, CINCO DE MAYO DEL AÑO DOS MIL DIECIOCHO

A LAS CINCO DE LA TARDE

ST. JUDE MELKITE CATHOLIC CHURCH

MIAMI, FLORIDA

Hispanic Heritage Invitation This elegant large (9" x 6") horizontal wedding invitation format is particularly suited to presenting the names of both sets of parents at the top, as is customary for Hispanic heritage weddings, and also pleasing for other traditions.

ב"ה

Roni and Bary Leeman

invite you to share in their happiness

as they celebrate the marriage of

Stacey Nicole

טלי

and

Gary Mark

הירש

son of Sandra ז"ל and Josh Liebesman

Sunday, the eleventh of July

two thousand and twenty-one

י בתמוז תשס"א

Chuppah at six o'clock in the evening

Dinner to follow

Winding Hollow Country Club

New Albany, Ohio

Orthodox Jewish Wedding In this invitation, the bride's and groom's names and the year are set in Hebrew. The groom's parents are included after his name. That his mother is deceased is indicated by the abbreviated Hebrew phrase following her name. The *bet hay* symbol in the upper right corner indicates that this card is a sacred document.

CELEBRATE SHABBAT WITH US

Friday evening Kabbalat Shabbat service
7 pm

Friday evening Shabbat dinner
8pm

Saturday morning services and Gary's Aufruf
9am

Kiddush Lunch
12 o'clock

Mincha Service
7:30 pm

Seudat Shlishit
(Shabbat's traditional third meal)
8 pm

Beth Jacob Synagogue
1223 College Avenue
Columbus, Ohio

Shabbat Card This invitation welcoming guests to a weekend of celebration was printed on a card smaller than the invitation and enclosed with it. Many weddings now include welcome dinners and other weekend activities to which all guests are invited.

Please respond by June 9th

M_____

Please indicate which events you will attend

_____ Friday evening Shabbat dinner

_____ Saturday Kiddush lunch

_____ Seudat Shlishit (Shabbat's traditional third meal)

_____ Sunday brunch

_____ We will need Shabbat weekend accommodations

_____ Stacy and Gary's wedding

_____ Declines with regret

Reply Card and Accommodations Card The reply card for this Jewish wedding celebration serves as an example for including replies to many wedding events taking place over an entire weekend. The accommodations card anticipates guests' needs for travel and lodging.

ACCOMMODATIONS

Rooms have been reserved for the Leeman-Liebesman wedding
at the following hotels:

COURTYARD BY MARRIOTT   THE WESTIN
Columbus Airport   Downtown Columbus
(800) 321-2211   (800) 937-8461

Complimentary shuttle service to wedding events will be provided.

Please make reservations at either hotel by June 1.

For travel arrangements please call Barbara
at People's Travel (800) 336-7662.

Please indicate your need for Shabbat accommodations on your reply
card, and we will be happy to arrange for you to stay with a family
in the community for the weekend.

OM SHREE GANESHAYA NAMAH

RAJIV AND MINA PATEL

REQUEST THE HONOUR OF YOUR PRESENCE TO GRACE THE AUSPICIOUS OCCASION
OF THE WEDDING CEREMONY OF THEIR BELOVED SON

Ramesh

GRANDSON OF THE LATE MR. DAYABHAI PATEL AND LATE MRS. BHAVNA PATEL

TO

Samantha

BELOVED DAUGHTER OF SATISH AND NILA GUPTA

SATURDAY, THE SECOND OF OCTOBER
TWO THOUSAND TWENTY-ONE

SLPS BANQUET HALL
555 SOUTH LAMAR STREET · DALLAS, TEXAS

BARAAT PROCESSION AT 9:30 AM   WEDDING CEREMONY AT 11:00 AM

FOLLOWED BY LUNCH

WITH BEST COMPLIMENTS FROM   NO BOXED GIFTS
PARAGBHAI AND MEERA PATEL
HITEN RAJIV PATEL
DUTT DARENDRA PATEL

South Asian Heritage Wedding invitation Indian families of all faith traditions may send two separate sets of wedding invitations: one from the bride's family and one from the groom's family, as shown here. Also customary is the inclusion of grandparents and other relatives as hosts or at the bottom of the invitation, after words such as *with the blessings of* or *with best compliments from.* Guests will be invited to multiple wedding events, on the main invitation or with additional enclosed cards. *No boxed gifts* is commonly included in the lower right corner.

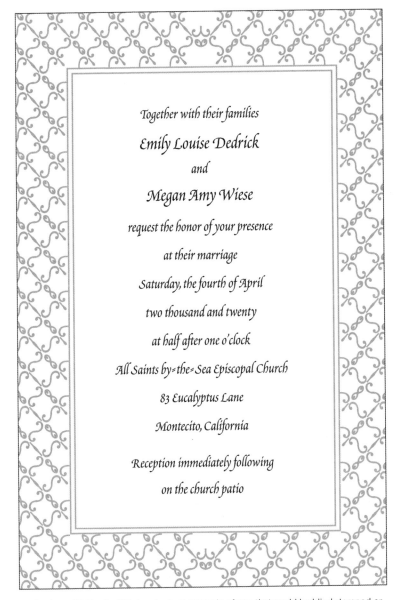

Together with their families

Emily Louise Dedrick

and

Megan Amy Wiese

request the honor of your presence

at their marriage

Saturday, the fourth of April

two thousand and twenty

at half after one o'clock

All Saints by⸗the⸗Sea Episcopal Church

83 Eucalyptus Lane

Montecito, California

Reception immediately following

on the church patio

Invitation with Border This border is an example of one that could be blind stamped or printed in any color. To maintain space around the type, a font that is somewhat condensed, such as an italic, is a good choice.

Together with their families

Audra Ricks Matthews

and

Rasheed Hakim Meadows

invite you to join in the celebation

of their marriage

Saturday, May 4, 2019

6:00 in the evening

Blaffer Art Museum

4173 Elgin Street

Houston, Texas

Informal Wedding invitation It's the wording, not the design, that makes this an informal wedding invitation.

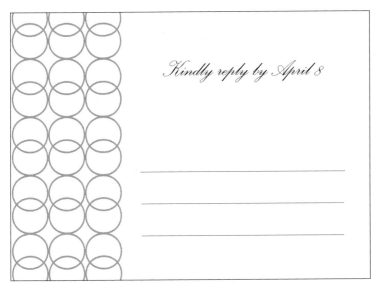

Reply Card and Thank You Folder The step-and-repeat double wedding rings design could be blind stamped or printed in any color. This design template, with a band of art at the bottom of the invitation and at the bottom or side of enclosure cards and thank you notes or folders, can work with a variety of styles of lines or bands (dotted, thick, thin) or patterns, or art such as floral designs from old engravings.

MR. & MRS. ALAN WADE CLARK

together with

MR. AND MRS. WILLIAM JASON CHAPMAN

request the pleasure of your company

at the marriage of their children

SARAH ANNE

and

VINCENT MARK

Friday, the twenty-third of June

two thousand twenty-one

at seven o'clock

THE SALT LICK

AUSTIN, TEXAS

Dinner and dancing to follow · Black tie

GREETINGS
Welcome to Austin!

FRIDAY NIGHT
REHEARSAL DINNER
(*by invitation*)
6:00 P.M. - Buses will leave both
W Hotel and Hilton Hotel
for the rehearsal dinner.

DAY OF LEISURE
SATURDAY FUN & RECREATION
Gypsy Picnic - Trailer Food Festival
Texas State Capital · Barton Springs · SoCo
2nd Street District · Texas Rowing Centre

THE BIG EVENT
WEDDING CEREMONY
4:00 P.M. - Buses will leave both
W Hotel and Hilton Hotel
for the Salt Lick ceremony
on Saturday at 5:30 P.M.

CELEBRATE
RECEPTION ON SATURDAY 6:00 P.M.
Dine & dance under the stars.
11:00 P.M. - first bus leaves The Salt Lick

FOND FAREWELL
Thank you for being a part of
our wedding celebration!

Tall Invitation with Activities Card This contemporary invitation for a black tie wedding welcomes guests to an itinerary of weekend events. The oval with the couple's initials and the star on the activites card were printed letterpress in school-bus yellow, with black type. SInce the colored shape will be debossed, the initials and the star between them will appear to be embossed, or raised. Both cards are about 4" x 9", the invitation double thick and the activities card single thickness.

Ms. Debra Martin and Mr. Robert Zacharopoulos

TOGETHER WITH THEIR DAUGHTERS

CLAIRE MARIE, CAROLINE ANNA AND MELINA ZOE

REQUEST THE HONOUR OF YOUR PRESENCE AT THEIR CELEBRATION OF MARRIAGE

SATURDAY, THE TWENTY-FIFTH OF MAY · TWO THOUSAND NINETEEN

ELEVEN O'CLOCK IN THE MORNING

SAINT DEMETRIOS GREEK ORTHODOX CHURCH

1217 NORTH AVENUE

WAUKEGAN, ILLINOIS

RECEPTION IMMEDIATELY FOLLOWING

THE HARRISON MANOR HOUSE

136 GREEN BAY ROAD

LAKE BLUFF, ILLINOIS

Second Wedding The bride and groom host this second wedding together with their children. This contemporary formal invitation uses both flush left and flush right type settings.

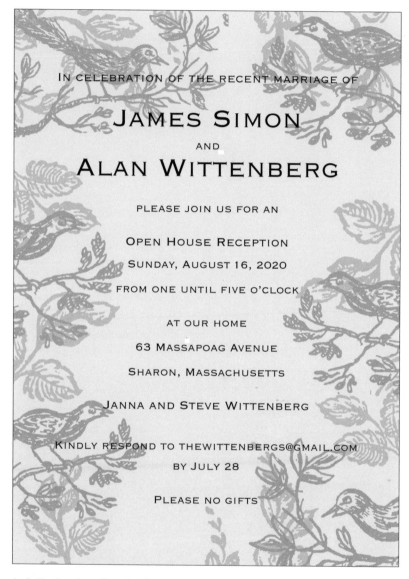

IN CELEBRATION OF THE RECENT MARRIAGE OF

JAMES SIMON

AND

ALAN WITTENBERG

PLEASE JOIN US FOR AN

OPEN HOUSE RECEPTION

SUNDAY, AUGUST 16, 2020

FROM ONE UNTIL FIVE O'CLOCK

AT OUR HOME

63 MASSAPOAG AVENUE

SHARON, MASSACHUSETTS

JANNA AND STEVE WITTENBERG

KINDLY RESPOND TO THEWITTENBERGS@GMAIL.COM

BY JULY 28

PLEASE NO GIFTS

Invitation to a Reception after the Wedding Date, given *in celebration of* the recent event. Note that the first-person point of view is used consistently throughout, with the hosts' names listed below the main invitation text. In this design, the bird art is printed in pale blue over paler blue leaves, and the type is dark warm gray. Art by Lauren McIntosh.

margaret and william kent

elaine and trevor marcus

are delighted to announce that their daughter and son

amanda delia kent & evan lee marcus

eloped to paris

friday, the twenty-second of April

and were married at the home of her parents

thursday, the twenty-first of june

two thousand eighteen

Wedding Announcement In this case, the event included an elopement, followed by a small wedding.

please save the date!

saturday, october 20, 2020

10.10.20

for the wedding of

mary allen & darryl redcloud

atlanta, georgia

invitation to follow

Save the Date Cards can introduce the style of the wedding invitations, or not, and may be accompanied by accommodations cards. Angela Welch calligraphy below.

Save the Date

November 30th, 2013

for the wedding

of

Maggie and Nolan

NEWPORT BEACH, CALIFORNIA · FORMAL INVITATION TO FOLLOW

Please share in our happiness

at a bridal shower

in honor of

Martina Lieberman

Sunday, April twenty-eighth

at one-thirty

Harmonie Club

Four East 60th Street

New York

Given with love by

Juliana* and Mikki

Say "I will"
(212) 955-2676*

Shower Invitation with Enclosure Card Bridal showers, engagement parties, and rehearsal dinners are all given *in honor of* the bride or the couple. This shower invitation demonstrates the use of an enclosure card to communicate a special message not included on the invitation, and presents a charming alternative to a *No gifts* request. The bouquet art is by Kelly Burke.

In lieu of a gift

your favorite recipe

would be most appreciated

Outer Envelope

Mr. and Mrs. Jason Brill
46 Fawn Street
Saranac Lake, New York
1 2 9 8 3

Inner Envelope

Mr. and Mrs. Brill
Spencer and Leo

Miss Catherine Torpey and Guest
4730 Kenmore Drive
Washington
District of Columbia
2 0 0 0 7

Single Envelope

Envelope Addresses These samples show a double envelope set and a single envelope.
Calligraphy by Gail Brill.

A. *Titles for Clergy, Government Officials, and Members of the Military*

For a couple, follow the Mr. and Mrs. order for spouses of equal rank or when the husband's rank is higher; list the woman first if her rank is the higher one.

Use of Titles for Clergy

If you are in doubt as to what title may be appropriate, you should consult the religious institution with which the clergy member is affiliated, the public information officer of the military base at which the person is based, the institution with which an official is affiliated, or the person in question.

BUDDHIST

There are several sects of Buddhism and regional traditions with different practices regarding titles. For example, the title *Roshi* may precede or follow the given name, and *Rimpoche* may also be spelled *Rinpoche*. It's best to consult the clergy member directly, or the institution with which he or she is associated.

CATHOLIC

An archbishop or bishop is referred to on an invitation and on an inner envelope with his title and surname, and on the outer envelope as *The Most Reverend* followed by his full name. An abbot and monsignor follow the same pattern, but with *Right Reverend* preceding his full name on the outer envelope. The titles *Brother, Sister*, and *Mother* are used with full names on outer envelopes and last names alone on inner envelopes, just like any other title. A priest is addressed with his full name and the title *The Reverend* on an outer envelope, and with the title *Father* followed by his last name on an inner envelope.

EPISCOPAL

For Episcopalian or Anglican clergy, use either *Mr.*, *Mrs.* or *Ms.* or substitute

Bishop, Archdeacon, Dean or *Canon* for *Mr., Mrs.* or *Ms.* on the invitation and the inner envelope. For the outer or single envelope, substitute the following titles for *Mr., Mrs.* or *Ms.*:

Bishop - *The Right Reverend*   Archdeacon - *The Venerable*

Dean - *The Very Reverend*   Canon - *The Reverend*

HINDU

The title most often used for a Hindu priest is *Pandit*, which is used with a full name on an invitation or envelope address, in place of *Mr.* Other titles may also be used for Hindu clergy, according to region and tradition.

ISLAMIC

Islamic titles such as *Imam* are used with full names, in place of *Mr.* when listed on a wedding invitation as a parent or for addressing envelopes.

JEWISH

Follow all the usual practices for listing hosts on invitations and for addressing envelopes, substituting *Rabbi* or *Cantor* for *Mr., Mrs.* or *Ms.* when applicable.

LATTER DAY SAINTS (MORMON)

The titles *President, Bishop, Elder, Brother,* and *Sister* are used with full names on outer envelopes and last names alone on inner envelopes, just like any other title. Titles are generally not used for the names on wedding invitations.

PROTESTANT

For protestant clergy, substitute *The Reverend* or *The Reverend Doctor* (for a minister with a doctorate) for *Mr., Mrs.* or *Ms.* when applicable and follow the usual forms.

Use of Titles for Government Officials

To correctly address foreign dignitaries, you should ask for guidance from their country's consulate.

For the following government officials, the form followed on the invitation, outer or single envelope, and inner envelope is this:

The President and Mrs.(or Mr.) Hopkins

The Vice President and Mrs.(or Mr.) Hopkins

Secretary of State (and all other cabinet members) *and Mrs.* (or *Mr.) Hopkins*

The Speaker of the House and Mrs. (or *Mr.) Hopkins*

The Chief Justice of the Supreme Court and Mrs. (or *Mr.) Hopkins*

ASSOCIATE JUSTICES

On an invitation or outer envelope, the title of *Madame Justice* or *Mr. Justice* is used for an associate justice of the Supreme Court. On the inner envelope, the title of *Justice* is used.

AMBASSADOR

For the invitation, use *Ambassador and Mrs., Ms.,* or *Mr.* For an outer or single envelope and also for the inner envelope, use *The Honorable*/full title (check with the embassy) *and Mrs., Ms.,* or *Mr.*

UNITED STATES SENATOR

For the invitation, use *Senator and Mrs. (or Mr.)*, for an outer or single envelope, *The Honorable* (full name) *and Mrs., Ms.,* or *Mr.*, and on the inner envelope, *Senator and Mrs., Ms.,* or *Mr.*

GOVERNOR

The governor of a state includes the state name on the invitation, as in *The Governor of Maine and Mrs., Ms.,* or *Mr.*, but it is omitted on the envelopes, which follow the pattern for the officials listed above.

MEMBER OF THE HOUSE OF REPRESENTATIVES
STATE SENATOR OR REPRESENTATIVE

These officials are addressed as *The Honorable* (full name) *and Mrs., Ms.,* or *Mr.* on an outer or single envelope, and as *Mr., Mrs.* or *Ms.* on the inner envelope or when hosting a wedding.

MAYOR

Envelopes are addressed to a mayor as *The Honorable* (full name) *and Mrs., Ms.,* or *Mr.* on an outer or single envelope, and as *Mr., Mrs.* or *Ms.* on the inner envelope. A mayor may host a wedding as *The Mayor of Springfield and Mrs., Ms.,* or *Mr. Hopkins.*

JUDGE

A judge is addressed as *The Honorable* (full name) *and Mrs., Ms.,* or *Mr.* on an outer or single envelope, as *Judge* on the inner envelope, and as *Judge* or *Mr.*, *Mrs.* or *Ms.* when hosting a wedding.

For further information on titles and ranking of federal officials, you can contact the Office of Protocol at The Department of State.

Military Titles

On an invitation, a host, bride, or groom may use a military rank as a title. The branch of service is not mentioned when the rank is used as a title for one member of a married couple, unless the names are listed individually on separate lines, connected by *and* before the name of the second (lower ranked) spouse. If both spouses share the same rank, they may be referred to collectively, as *The Colonels* (last name), for example.

The rank of an officer is placed before a name, with the branch of service in the next line. For a junior officer, the rank is listed in the second line, ahead of the branch of service. A noncommissioned officer or enlisted man or woman does not use a title, but lists the name of the branch of service in a line following his or her name. A member of the reserves doesn't list rank or branch of service unless on active duty.

In addressing envelopes to members of the military, substitute a rank for *Mr.*, *Mrs.* or *Ms.* and follow the normal forms. In married couples, the spouse with the higher rank should be listed first. For complete information on military rank, the Public Information Officer at the nearest military base should be able to help you.

Other Titles

Commercial airline pilots are usually given the honor of the title *Captain*, even though they do not hold military rank. Persons of rank in police and fire departments should also be addressed with their rank, such as *Captain* or *Commissioner*.

B. *How to Line Envelopes*

There are three main steps for lining envelopes: making the template; cutting the lining paper (usually tissue); and gluing the liners into the envelopes. You'll need a piece of cardboard somewhat larger than your envelope, your lining paper, a razor blade such as an X-ACTO knife, a cutting mat (preferably self-healing), a pencil, a ruler, and a glue stick—the paste kind, not the kind that dispenses liquid glue. Make sure you start with a few extra envelopes.

1) Make the Template

To make the template, use the pencil to draw around your envelope on the cardboard. Then use a ruler to draw a new outline inside the outline you made from the envelope itself. The inner outline will be the template for the liner. For a pointed flap envelope, it should be drawn about 1/2 inch inside the envelope outline on the sides and flap, and reach the bottom of the envelope. For a square-flap envelope, cut it about 1/4 inch narrower on the sides, 1/2 inch from the top edge of the flap, and then follow the taper of the flap to the top. It also should reach the bottom of the envelope. Cut out the cardboard along the inner line that you've drawn to create the template.

shaded areas show liner

2) Cut One Liner and Test it

Using the razor blade, cut around your template through a piece of liner paper (do this on the self-healing cutting mat, cardboard, or another expendable surface). Slip this liner into your envelope, letting it reach the bottom of the envelope. If you like how it looks, your template is fine; if not, make adjustments to the template. Apply glue along the top (flap) edge of the liner paper on the side that will be against the envelope. Slide it into the envelope, being careful to center it and letting it reach the bottom, and then press the glued surface against the envelope. Close it and then open it again. If you still like what you see, you're ready to go on. If the liner seems too large, trim your template. If the liner seems too small, you'll have to cut a new, larger template.

3) Cut All the Liners

You should be able to cut through at least a few sheets of liner paper at a time with a sharp razor blade, using your template as a guide.

4) Install the Liners

Follow the procedure describe above when you tested your first liner, or try placing a liner in an envelope first, folding the flap and creasing the liner. Then open the envelope, fold the liner toward you along the crease, and apply the glue. Either fold the envelope flap down again or unfold the liner and press it against the open flap. Try a few each way and see what works best for you.

C. *Sources*

Wedding Invitations

There are too many purveyors of wedding invitations at all price levels and styles, and too many more coming into and leaving the market to list them all here. The best thing to do is to visit a local stationer and look at sample albums. You won't see absolutely everything available at any one store, but most stores have a wide selection to choose from. Large national companies may have sample albums in many stores in your community, while a small company like mine has a much smaller distribution and may not have a sample album in any stores in your town.

Wedding magazines can help you find invitation companies that are sold through stationery stores, online, or mail order. You'll see a wide range of advertisements for wedding invitations, all of them with the addresses of websites you can visit for more information, and some of them, generally mail-order companies, with postcards you can send in for samples. *Martha Stewart Weddings* has led the way with stationery coverage, and is still the most complete. They don't just report the trends, they often create them. In addition to showing the work of many professionals, their writers and designers continually present fresh ideas that you can incorporate into your wedding stationery yourself.

It's hard to find a good listing of invitation sources on the internet. Websites presenting themselves as resources seem mostly to offer only paid links, and/or links to their "partners" (the same thing), and invitations posted on internet bulletin boards are often not clearly sourced or easily available. There are many online vendors offering wedding invitations, but you will need to order samples to assess the quality of the products, and may not have any recourse if you are not happy with what you receive. Some stationery stores have websites, and some of them show the invitation lines they offer, sometimes with links to the informational websites of those companies.

Stationers

If you don't know of a good local stationer, you might find one by looking at advertisements for wedding invitations in national magazines. Many of those advertisers have informational websites you may visit to learn about their offerings, with directories of retail stores you may visit to see sample albums and for personal assistance in placing your order.

Calligraphers

You can find a calligrapher through your stationer or wedding planner, or online through organizations such as the Society of Scribes.

www.societyofscribes.org

The calligraphers whose work is shown in this book are listed below.

Gail Brill (pages 29, 73) gailbrilldesign@gmail.com or 518-586-1063

Mo Seder (page 73) Union Street Papery, San Francisco, 415-563-0200

Lauren McIntosh (page 73) laurenmcswan@hotmail.com

Maria Helena Hoksch (page 73, 102) www.calligraphybymariahelena.com or 504-363-9129

Angela Welch (page 104, 120) http://www.penandpauper.com, 229-243-0045

Type and Type Ornaments

The best sources for type and typographical ornaments can be found online at these addresses:

www.typography.com *(Hoefler & Co.)*

www.adobe.com

www.emigre.com

www.fontbureau.com

www.myfonts.com *this one markets fonts from many different creators*

www.winsornewton.com *their Type Embellishment Fonts contain a variety of typographical ornaments*

Clip Art

The offerings of clip art on the internet are staggering. Much of it is awful, and I don't know how you can wade through all the muck to find the good stuff. I think the best quality source overall is www.doverpublications.com. You'll find their books and CDs at many art supply and bookstores as well. They are best for botanical subjects and ornaments such as headbands and borders in many artistic traditions. Their art is of good quality and copyright free. One problem with clip art is that it might not always be available at the high resolution needed for high-quality engraving or letterpress; 300 or 600 dpi might be fine for offset or digital printing, but that will look pixelated when printed letterpress or engraved. If you can't get the art at 1200 dpi, you can try outlining it in Illustrator, or otherwise redraw it.

Ribbons and Papers

I think it's best to shop at your local stationery, paper or art supply store for these materials. Art schools often have stores open to the general public, carrying a wide selection of papers and other artists' materials. So much of the quality of paper or ribbon is in the feel, which you can't get at all from a catalog or over the internet, and colors are usually not represented accurately enough in books, magazines, catalogs, or computer screens to make real-world color choices. Many stationery and paper stores carry wide selections of these materials and can also place special orders from their sample books for you, prepaid and nonreturnable.

MIDORI (www.midoriribbon.com) is one of the best ribbon suppliers, but they don't sell directly to individuals. If you like something you see on their website, you should contact them for a store near you that carries their products. That store might have the ribbon you like or be able to add it to their next order for you.

DANIEL SMITH in Seattle is a well-known purveyor of papers and other artists' materials. They have a catalog and you can also order from them online. www.danielsmith.com

APEC is a great source for glassine and translucent vellum envelopes and sheets. www.apecenvelopes.com

Folders, Jackets, and Wraps

You can make your own wraps and simple folders with papers you find at art supply stores. Jackets, pocket folders, and other die-cut enclosures which you can use to customize a simple invitation design are carried by many stationers, and you can also find them from online sources.